PRAISE FOR THE AUTHOR

"John Chase, MD, an orthopaedic surgeon for more than three decades, practiced while orthopaedic surgery made remarkable advances. During Dr. Chase's career, recovery time for injured patients dramatically shortened, worn out joints are now replaced and career ending sports injuries are now treated with minimally invasive surgery allowing the athlete to return to full capability. Dr. Chase practiced orthopaedic surgery during this transition and participated in the amazing advancements made in the care of the musculoskeletal system. His observations and commentary provide an insider's view of the practice of orthopaedic surgery."

Dempsey Springfield, MD

"It was only after becoming a medical student that I learned the stereotype associated with orthopaedic surgeons: brash, brawny and arrogant men with a fix-it mentality and a predilection for sports metaphors. But, as a pediatric patient and then a college-aged mentee, the Dr. Chase I grew to respect and admire simply shattered the stereotype. As an undergraduate student shadowing at his side, Dr. Chase taught me to value patient's narratives, respect the art of the physical exam, continually seek self-improvement, and always provide comfort, even when cure wasn't possible. I am a better internist today thanks to the mentoring and teaching of this orthopaedic surgeon."

Beth Ann Yakes, MD, Associate Professor of Medicine, Vanderbilt University Medical Center; Associate Program Director, Internal Medicine Residency Program, Vanderbilt University Medical Center

"I grew up learning from and admiring Dr. Chase. He was one of the main individuals who inspired me to pursue a career in medicine. As I considered my future goals, he became a mentor. Some of my most treasured experiences came from my time with him. It was wonderful to see someone so passionate about their work, and who loved to teach. Dr. Chase has a way about him, making people feel valued and included. He brought life and fun to medicine and encouraged me to continue pursuing my goals. I am thankful to have learned from him."

Morgan Sanders, MD, Pediatric Resident

"Dr. John Chase has taken care of several members of my family with kindness, gentleness, love and expertise in his profession. He performed knee surgery on my husband, corrected a hyperextended leg on our son, and saved our daughter's leg after an auto accident. Her leg had atrophied tendons from a delay in getting needed surgery at the hospital she was taken to. Dr. Chase has a heart full of compassion, a brain to think things through, and technique to accomplish a cure for his patients. Our family will always think of him with love, affection and prayers for his future and his family."

Rita Rackley, Former Patient

"I was lucky enough to work alongside Dr. Chase for nine years. He quickly became a wonderful mentor, role model and friend to me. Dr. Chase spent time listening carefully to his patients, and always made decisions that had their best interest in mind. He taught me different ways to think and assess our patients, and we formed a great team. My favorite memories of clinic with him are all the jokes, funny stories, and of course his quick wit and sense of humor. I was fortunate to learn from him and I am forever grateful for his mentorship."

Sarah Colandreo, PT, DPT, CMPT, OCS

"John Chase M.D. practiced Orthopaedic Surgery for over 30 years. He was well regarded by his peers and patients alike for his personal approach, orthopedic knowledge and practical solutions to orthopedic problems. He enjoyed close working relationships with his patients, who benefited greatly from his care and expertise. Many medical students, mid-level providers, nursing staff and para-professionals were carefully and expertly mentored during his career. I was one of the mid-level providers that was fortunate to benefit from his mentorship. Working with Dr. Chase in the office or the surgical suite allowed me to observe firsthand the wonderful care that his patients received."

Skip Repass, Physician's Assistant

YOU WHAT?!

YOU WHAT?!

Humorous Stories, Cautionary Tales, and
Unexpected Insights About A Career in Medicine

JOHN CHASE, MD

Illustrations by Kathy Heath

THRONE
PUBLISHING GROUP

ISBN Softcover: 978-1-949550-45-0
Ebook ISBN: 978-1-949550-46-7

Printed in the United States of America.

Cover Design: Heidi Caperton
Lead Writer: John Chase, MD
Editor: Marguerite Bonnett
Proofing Editor: Claire Obermarck
Publishing Manager: Janet Pomeroy

Although the author and publisher have made every effort to ensure that the information and advice in this book was correct and accurate at press time, the author and publisher do not assume and hereby disclaim any liability to any party for any loss, damage, or disruption caused from acting upon the information in this book or by errors or omissions, whether such errors or omissions result from negligence, accident, or any other cause.

Throne Publishing Group
1601 East 69th St N Suite 306
Sioux Falls, SD 57108
ThronePG.com

DEDICATION

I dedicate this book to my family.

To my wife Marian. I could not have done this without you. Thanks for sticking with me through the "bumps in the road." I love you!

To Megan, Sarah, and Anna and their families. You are my raison d'etre (reasons for living). I love you all!

ACKNOWLEDGMENTS

I'd like to thank Kathy Heath for her brilliant illustrations that perfectly capture in pictures what I was trying to pass along in text. You have added greatly to this book.

Thank you, Meredith Mallory, for implanting the idea in my brain to write this book.

Thanks to Mike MacMillan and Skip Repass for their multiple contributions to the subject matter, and for the stories, and anecdotes throughout this book.

Great appreciation to the mentors in my life, both medical and not. Much of what I pass along was inspired by you.

Much recognition to our office staff, hospital staff, surgery center staff, trainers and therapists that I have worked with who are dedicated to good patient care without the recognition that physicians get. What you all do so well is make it possible for us to do our jobs. You make us look good. I have enjoyed working with you immensely.

And finally my great appreciation to Throne Publishing— Jeremy Brown, Ryan Hultgren, Janet Pomeroy, Heidi Caperton, and Marguerite Bonnett for helping me organize many random thoughts into a hopefully entertaining and coherent book with some lessons for those new to the medical fields.

John Chase

TABLE OF CONTENTS

PART 2: YOUR REWARDS

PART 3: YOUR LIFE

FORWARD

John Chase is one of the few surgeons I know who made it through medical school, internship, Orthopaedic residency, and a busy Orthopaedic practice without drinking coffee. I would never have thought this possible except I witnessed him going through these experiences. I survived only by the grace of Java.

How did he do that? In John's case, he pulled it off through a superhero like positive attitude, a dedication to the wellbeing of others, a superb memory, and an unnatural ability to be liked by almost everyone he met. Somehow, he took the rigorous training experience that most surgeons look back on like 'boot camp meets root canal' and made it feel like a memorable, challenging adventure. It was my good fortune to have him as a colleague during these trying times.

As we traveled through internship, residency, employment and later raising families, little did I know that John was leveraging his hard drive like memory with notes and memorabilia. I might have been a little more judicious in my alcohol lubricated rants about the various personalities and institutions we encountered had I known a book was being planned. Nevertheless, the book has arrived.

The journey is told in anecdotes, recollections, and nostalgic stories that recall the pre-digital pioneer days of paper charts and patient wards and carries the reader through to modern telemedicine and mega-hospitals. The constant themes, however, are the human stories of patients' experiences, doctor-patient travails, and the reality-show-like drama of the day-to-day surgical life-style.

The individual vignettes put a spotlight on moments that occur almost daily in the hectic schedule of a surgeon going from training into a large orthopaedic practice. The early stories recall a time when medicine was an art, not a business. Especially poignant for me were the recollections of daily teaching conferences where naïve trainees were put in the crucible of the 'Case Presentation' and forced to go head-to-head and toe-to-toe to defend their knowledge of patient care with senior faculty members. It points out how, in the new age of Dr. Google and Wikipedia, the teaching of critical thinking is being sacrificed on the altar of the search engine.

While it delivers on many levels, it is the collection of stories itself that leaves a greater overall impression. The glimpses of the past reveal how medicine is being transformed and how this one doctor tried to carry on the traditions of the doctor-patient relationship as the world of medicine evolved into numbers, reimbursement codes, and treatment pathways.

This book should serve as a caution during this pivotal time in medicine not to abandon the interpersonal relationship of medical care. As the pandemic forces us into telemedicine and artificial intelligence takes over the role of medical decision making, we need to be reminded of the human element of medicine. Hopefully, the readers of this book will be reminded of the universal question of patient care: "How would you want your mother or father to be treated?"

Mike MacMillan
Retired Orthopaedic Spine Surgeon

INTRODUCTION

"Dr. Chase, with all these stories, you should write a book!" said Meredith, my X-ray technician. I said, "Maybe I will!"

That started me compiling stories of the sometimes unbelievable things that people have done and said over the course of practicing orthopaedic surgery for 40 years.

My original intent was to relay the silly and absurd moments ("YOU WHAT?"), but as I was writing, I found myself talking to my medical students, trying to share my life experience to help smooth their way through medical school and into practicing medicine. So, along with the silly and the absurd, I include some practical advice about how to be successful, have fun and take care of your patients without missing out on what really matters in life.

So here are stories from my journey to laugh at for those in medicine, insights for those who are not in the medical field, and lessons for young people just starting down the medical path.

Enjoy!

PART I

YOUR PRACTICE

CHAPTER 1
YOUR FIRST THREE YEARS

YOU Want Me to Do WHAT?

"I made it. My dream has come true. Now there is no one telling me what to do. Finally!" I remember that feeling well.

The big day arrived! It was my first day in practice of orthopaedic surgery. I had been through four years of college, four years of medical school and six years of residency. That's a lot of delayed gratification! Doctors are very good at delayed gratification.

For young doctors starting out, that's an extra ten years of delayed gratification while your college classmates are out working, traveling, making money, and starting a family. All while you are killing yourself with very long hours and very low pay for your educational level.

You feel deprived.

To make matters worse, throughout your entire residency, your attending physician, (your boss, who you may or may not like or respect) has been telling you what decisions to make with patients, how to do the surgery, and even, at times, how to behave.

You are tired of it.

Your residency has ended and you are finally going into practice where you can be your own boss. Now, you have that independence you have been pining for for years.

Finally.

But moving from residency to practice was not the utopia of independence I had imagined.

My First Day in the Office

My first day in the office was exciting. I was confident but nervous. I knew the orthopaedic stuff. It was everything else I didn't know. Here's how things went down.

Patients can show up with anything because I am the new guy. I don't have any of my own patients and I am the path of least resistance when they call. Patients are great. But... How do I actually do this? What hospital do I go to? What doctors should I use for consultants? Who can help me with these things? I don't want to bother my partners with these trivial things.

The Nurses are Your Friend

The nurses! They can help me with these things. And I learned a very important lesson right out of the gate. It was July of 1980 and I had just started my internship. The nurses in the surgical intensive care unit (ICU) had been very nice, very helpful (probably because I looked to be ten years old). I was writing my notes and the nurses were bustling around doing their ICU tasks when all of a sudden, the neurosurgeons barge into the ICU on rounds and immediately start barking orders.

This group was a notorious bunch of jerks and very quickly reinforced that impression. Suddenly, all the nurses disappeared, frantically busy with tasks that took them as far away as possible from these schmucks. I remember thinking, "There is a lesson to be learned here!"

I'm convinced that a lot of doctors are mean to everybody they work with because they try to make themselves feel bigger by belittling those around them. Probably because of insecurity.

I have said for years that the best reflection of a person's character is how they treat the people around them that they think can't do anything for them. Lots of people are nice when there is something in it for them.

Be nice to the nurses. Don't piss off the nurses. They will do their jobs as nurses because they are professionals and they care about the patients. But, if they don't hate you, they can make your life much easier. Treat them decently and with respect, because a lot of doctors don't.

My First Surgery Patient

"First day in the office. This is what I was meant to do. Bring them on!"

On my first day, Mary showed up in the office with her daughter Joan. (I am very good at remembering names.) She had a bad broken wrist that needed to be fixed. I recommended that she have an external fixator placed in surgery that week. "I got this!" Then I thought, "Let me check with the attending physician before we get it scheduled." Wait a minute, there is no attending! I am my own boss! Suddenly, anxiety and doubt set in. I've been waiting all this time to be on my own and now it's here. Is this the right thing to do?

Then, there are all these questions from my patient. "Is that the only way to do it?" "No ma'am." "Is that the best way to do this?" "I believe so." "Pins in my wrist?" "Yes ma'am." "Are you old enough to do this?" ("Of course, I am!") "Yes, ma'am, I am a board eligible Orthopaedic surgeon." (What I didn't say was this is my first surgery on my own.)

She went on and on and I patiently answered her multitude of questions. She was a real worry wart. We finally agreed to get the surgery scheduled for that week.

"THEY WHAT?" I can't believe these people are really going to do what I recommend. Astonishing! And now, Mr. Big Shot, Dr. Independent… I now have all these questions. This is way harder than I planned! All the little details that go along with surgery were always somebody else's responsibility during my residency. Now it's all mine!

Thankfully, that's when the nurses kicked in. "Here are the papers you need to fill out." "I'll call Sylvia to come get it scheduled." "Here is the phone number for the rep for the external fixator that the other doctors like best." The nurses are your friend.

So, we did the surgery. And with external pins in her wrist, it was painful, for both of us! She had lots of questions. Every time! But everything worked out ok. She (and her daughter and grandson and other family members) came back to see me a number of times over the years and we made a real connection. I like to think of it as a musculoskeletal family practice. In fact, 30 years later when Mary fractured her patella (kneecap), she and Joan came back and they wanted me to do her surgery. Pretty cool!

As I was starting my practice, I realized that, despite the fact I had been training for six years, I didn't know everything! (I didn't?) One of our faculty at the University of Florida Orthopaedic Residency, Dempsey Springfield, warned us we wouldn't see everything in residency and what we were there for was to learn how to think and use the principles of the musculoskeletal system and surgery to develop an approach and handle the problem. He was a great teacher.

I knew right away I needed some advice. But that can be hard to admit. It takes a strong ego to become a surgeon. I'm supposed to be this hotshot new partner with new techniques and ideas. I don't want other people to think I don't know what I am doing. It's embarrassing, as well as damaging to my ego.

This is why a lot of young surgeons seem arrogant. Some of them really are. But some of them just don't want to look like they don't know what they are doing. If a nurse mentions something that might help, she is likely to get her head bitten off with a sharp, "I'm the doctor here. I don't need any advice from a nurse!" Or, if a nurse dares to say, "I have seen Dr. Barnett do it this way," she could be slapped with a terse, "Well, Dr. Barnett is not here now, is he?" Only someone "realistically confident" can accept advice, particularly in the operating room.

Ask for Advice

The secret is to "Get a guy." (Good advice for life, as well.) Find somebody you can go to who understands young people don't know everything. Go to a quiet place, away from everybody else, where you can ask questions. Find someone who will give you good advice and won't blab to everybody.

Greg Munson was that guy for me, even though we didn't do the same type of surgery. Often, the medical issues are not the difficult ones. It's the other things, like how do you handle the difficult patient or what consultant should I use? You may need help with political issues (local MD stuff, not Republican and Democrat stuff). Another great question is "Who can I trust and who should I watch out for?"

There are always people to watch out for. Some are just not good people. You are going to have to learn how to deal with them. The bad behavior of doctors has been tolerated for way too long, especially in the operating room (OR). Find out who the worst ones are and stay clear of them as best you can. Oh, and don't become one of them!

CHAPTER 2
BEING IN PRACTICE

In order to get to that first day in practice, you have to find one you like. Let's go through the process of picking a practice to join. How do you do that? I am focusing on private practice, not an academic practice or research. There are other books written about that.

First, you have to decide where you and your family (if there is one to consider) want to live and what kind of practice you want to have. Then there are the questions you ask yourself: How do I get paid? How much? What about being on call? When do I become a partner? How much is that buy-in? Where will I work? What are the hours? What about drive time? How bad is the traffic? What kind of independence do I have or will "somebody" (an administrator, a doctor or group of them) be telling me what to do? How many patients am I expected to see and how many surgeries am I expected to do? The list is endless.

Choosing A Practice

The biggest problem of choosing a practice is that you are doing this during your residency-the time in your life that you have the least "free time." You are trying to learn, get increasing graduating responsibility, you're on call frequently and consequently sleep deprived. If you have a relationship or are married, that demands your time. And if you have kids, you want (hopefully) to be involved in their lives. Where is the time to choose a practice?

Besides choosing a spouse, choosing your practice is the most important decision you will make as a doctor. You are actually choosing the people you will be married to in your practice. These people will have more to do with your happiness in life than anybody, except your spouse.

It's terrible how most of us do it. You might look at a few lists of practices who are looking to add someone new. (Are they really? Or are they just trying to get more bodies to take call and really don't want to give up any of their practice?) You ask your faculty. You send out letters. Basically, you are self-initiating a job interview. And you have never been trained for this. Certainly nothing in residency prepares you for this.

Then you schedule a visit to view the practice. One visit is not enough, but being realistic, that is probably all you are going to get. What if you want to visit several practices?

In my case, I made visits to several places. We were looking in the Midwest, so I requested an interview with a group in St. Louis that looked interesting. But it was strange. They didn't offer to pay for my expenses for my wife and I to visit there. Okay, maybe times were bad or they were just cheap. We went through the whole interview and at the end they said, "Well, we weren't really looking to take on somebody new." "YOU WHAT?" Then why did you have me take the time and expense to interview?" Jerks.

I had another visit with a practice tour and a scheduled dinner with all the partners. Really? A two-hour dinner sitting in the middle of a big table and the only people you have a chance to have any kind of a conversation with are those you are directly adjacent to? On top of that, Marian was pregnant with our second child, Sarah, when we interviewed. She had afternoon and evening nausea, not morning sickness. During dinner, she started to feel bad and needed to leave, but I couldn't leave. This was my interview! One of the younger partners offered to take her back to the hotel in his prized Jaguar. I was thinking to myself, "Please Dear, don't throw up in his Jaguar or I'll never get this job." She was a trooper. She didn't puke until she got into the hotel room.

That's how I chose the people I would be married to for 30 years? Yes. That's the group I joined. Crazy. It's a crapshoot! When you join a medical practice, that means doctors. (Not a coincidence.) And doctors can be a difficult group to deal with. Here's what you want to look out for.

Choose Good People

You want to be in practice with "good people." That includes your administrator. One of the patients came to our chief executive officer (CEO) to complain about a particular doctor. He was late, they had to wait forever, and a list of other things to be unhappy about. (There are some people you just can't please.) After a litany of complaints, this patient said, "And nobody told me he was black." Our CEO's response was "He is? Nobody told me either." Jay was a great guy.

But the main group you want to make sure are "good people" is the other doctors you will be in practice with: your partners. Doctors are generally driven, type A personalities. It's almost required to even get into medical school. You also need the grades. Really good ones. Unless you are innately brilliant. And even if you are, you still have to work very hard to get those grades. That involves time buried studying, and lots of it.

Studying means time spent away from interacting with people in college and medical school. There's not a lot of time to develop social skills. Those are not rewarded in pre-med. Time other students spend learning how to deal with all kinds of people through activities, clubs, partying and volunteering are not re-warded to pre-meds and medical students. Only grades are. Is it any wonder that so many doctors don't have much personality? Doctors are a difficult group and you can blame a lot of that on medical school.

Residencies, depending upon what kind and where, can be some of the most inhumane experiences this side of third world dicta-tors. One day, as I was writing my notes on the pediatric floor, I heard a pediatric intern ask her senior resident, "Why are those neurosurgery residents so mean?" The response was, "Well, if you take a dog, a not too nice dog to start with, tie it up and beat it every day for five years, it is going to get mean!"

I told my three daughters, Megan, Sarah and Anna, "If you ever go out with a doctor, it should be in spite of the fact that he is a doctor, not because he's a doctor." Doctors are no prize! And these are the people you will be married to for 30 years. So, choose wisely.

Marian and I chose to go where we did because we liked the lo-cation, the clinic had been there a long time and had a great rep-utation. I liked the doctors I met, and felt that the people, there at the time, would be fair. It wasn't a trauma center and the call was spread out among ten people. I also felt that I didn't have to make these doctors my only social group and belong to their country club. Also, one of them was wearing a short-sleeved shirt (which I did) and I didn't feel like I was going to have to dress or behave in a certain way because of where I worked. It may sound like a dumb factor, but it seemed important to me at the time.

Practice Divorces

It's a wonder there aren't more "practice divorces" than there are. You are making big decisions about finances and your future with these people. You hope they are fair, but you don't know. The best way to find out what the people are like that you will be working with is to ask the nurses and the people who work with the doctors. (Comes up again doesn't it? The nurses always know what you are really like.) But I don't know a great way to ask. Inevitably, when there is a practice divorce, it is usually due to personality problems, not professional competence.

Tips for Being in Practice

Tip #1 Take Care of Your Family

This career can be hard on families. Difficulties include time away from the family, the stress (internal and external), AND pressure to build your practice. Medical families have a high rate of divorce.

I always felt family was important. I believe that you can't create quality time. Quality time just happens and you have no idea when it will happen. You can't make it happen on a Sunday trip to the zoo. It happens when you least expect it and the best chance of creating it is when you have "quantity time." It might be when you are reading a story to your kids or at dinner with nothing special going on. If you are never home for dinner, those moments don't happen. Some of my best moments with my three daughters were cranking tunes and crazy dancing after dinner.

The moment this became very clear was when we were having dinner with one of my older partners, who, at age 60, was starting a new family with young kids. He told my wife, "I don't think men can become good fathers until they are at least 60." My wife, Marian, said to me later, "What he meant is that he couldn't give a crap about being a father until he was at least 60! I'll bet his first set of kids wouldn't appreciate hearing that comment."

I always tried to make the time to be at all my kids events. It didn't always happen. When you are on call, your time is not yours. ER calls with an emergency and you have to go. No questions.

Doctors are on the phone all the time. Early on, I couldn't leave home because there were no cell phones. I had to always be near a landline. And the first thing I did when I walked into any location was to find the location of a phone where I could have a quiet conversation.

My kids may not have realized I was a doctor because I was almost always there. (Now, they may not have wanted me there, yelling at referees or providing "suggestions" for their event that day.) It wasn't until later that they found out, that was not the norm. In order to do that, I had to arrange schedules so I could get out early (or try like hell). This lowered the number of patients I could see. (Initially, that was skin off only my own nose. I produced less, so I made less. That's fair. Later in my career, that was not tolerated and I paid for it, literally and figuratively.) Don't get yourself in a practice where the pressure for production creates pressure and stress you may not want to or are incapable of handling. It's hard to know and ferret that out in advance. Just be aware. If money is all they talk about in your interview, then you should be suspicious.

Tip #2 Get Out of Debt

Get out of debt as soon as you can. And don't get yourself into it even more. One of my guiding principles is to never take on debt unless 1) Somebody else is paying part of it, i.e., the government by making some of it tax deductible, such as interest on home a mortgage or two) You are investing in yourself, i.e., school, education etc. And get out of it at soon as you can. It is very freeing.

Have an emergency reserve fund of three to four months of expenses in a liquid form. So when the inevitable disaster happens, you can weather it, rather than panicking and dipping into your retirement or taking on more debt. (Doctors can almost always get loans. You're a doctor, for heaven's sake.)

Long before I got there, many of my partners fell hook line and sinker for a Ponzi scheme. The office manager introduced them to this "hot deal" (always be suspicious of a ``hot deal") where the government was going to require ice machines to package all ice in commercial facilities (hotels, etc.) in plastic for hygiene reasons. Of course, they could get in on this deal early and all it would take was some significant early investment capital. Some of them even took out money from their retirement accounts (at a penalty) because it was such a sure thing. Boom! It was a classic Ponzi scheme and they lost their proverbial shirts. Don't do that!

I know doctors who've been in practice for years who are living paycheck to paycheck. No doctor has an income problem. If you don't have enough money, you have a spending problem.

Tip #3. Reduce Stress

Find a way to cut down on your stress. It's better for your coronary arteries and stomach lining. This job is stressful enough. There are emergencies, surgeries that are difficult or challenging, and threats of potential lawsuits with every patient you see. Figure out a way to cut down on the things that cause you stress.

When my daughter, Sarah, was about five years old, she was playing down the street with the daughter of one of my partners. Jim came in and said, "How's your Dad doing today?"

She replied, "Not very good. He's on call!" (I'm convinced that was a major reason none of my three children went into medicine after all those years of listening to me bitch about being on call.)

Jim said, "Yeah, I'm not in a very good mood when I am on call either."

Totally unsolicited, she said "Yeah, but what really gets my Dad in a bad mood is when he has to talk to lawyers!" When my five-year-old knows how much I hate dealing with lawyers from sitting at the dinner table, then I need to do something to cut that down.

So, I stopped taking all referrals from lawyers and tried to cancel any appointments for new patients when I saw they had legal representation. If they have a lawyer before they see the doctor, then you know: 1) This it is not an emergency, and 2) Their focus is their legal case, not getting better.

Tip #4 Manage Your Time

I am pathologically punctual. Not being on time for something makes me very uneasy. (I know what you're thinking. Are you sure I am a real doctor?) I hate to get behind at the office. It seems like a small thing to get stressed about because all doctors get behind. I always start on time, but inevitably, things happen that mess with the schedule. There are a myriad of reasons and I have spent years trying to hone that to keep it to a minimum.

There is no right way, but I did the right thing for me. Sometimes, you reduce internal stress and then it creates external stress or vice versa. There is no way to make this job stressless, but figure out what causes your stress and try to limit it.

Tip #5 Limit Your Exposure to Jerks

You can't entirely do this. There are too many out there. But try to keep your exposure to the barest of minimums. One of my favorite quotes comes from Dabo Swinney, head football coach at Clemson University. He said, "I've learned not to worry about criticism from people who I wouldn't otherwise seek out their advice." Enough said.

Tip #6 Forgive

Forgiveness is very good advice that I have tried to live by, but I have rarely been successful. I'm better at letting it recede than actually forgiving. But I like the concept and I recommend it. Because, anger really will eat you up inside.

Tip #7 Take Your Vacations

For years I have heard my patients say, "Doc, we had all these plans to travel after we retired and now all we do is go to doctor's visits."

We are not promised anything. You could die tomorrow. Overused cliché, I know. But it happened to a friend and former partner of mine. Greg actually retired from our practice. He was the only doctor in 30 years from our practice to manage that. Everybody else either died from a plane crash (we had three of those), got cancer, went out on "sudden" disability, or got in trouble and had to stop practicing. Greg had planned on doing some traveling, visiting family and all the things you do when you are retired.

One day, he was admitted to the hospital for some routine tests. He was fine and actually reviewing some legal cases for consultation when he suddenly got a headache and went unconscious. Doctors were unable to revive him and emergency surgery for a sudden brain bleed couldn't save him. It was all a total surprise. Lesson learned. Take those trips while you can and don't wait until you are retired. You might not be here.

Now, let's go visit the wonderland of what it's like "seeing patients." They are the reason you go into this business, rather than just doing research.

CHAPTER 3
SEEING PATIENTS

Patients frequently come in and say, "Doc, it's just hell getting old." And our standard response is, "Well, it's better than the alternative." Chuckle, chuckle. But one of my favorite patients had the final come back when she replied, "I suppose you are right. It's better to be seen than to be viewed."

As I started seeing patients on my own, I began to learn some things. Some patients are wonderful people who come to you with a problem, you fix it, they get better and you have a decades-long relationship with them. And some patients are not so nice to deal with. Some are not compliant, some lie and some are a major risk for you. Here are a few stories to give you an idea of what a new doctor might encounter.

My Top "YOU WHAT?" Moments with Patients

Noncompliance

Kids, by definition, are going to be non-compliant. Just plan on it. They are not bad, they are just kids. We used to say in residency, "Pediatric orthopaedics is like veterinary medicine. They will do none of what you tell them to do." That is why you will put kids in casts so they can't do what you don't want them to do.

I saw a nine-year-old neighbor for a fractured leg, put him in a cast and told him not to walk on it. I drove home that evening and there he was, in the driveway, playing basketball. "He's doing WHAT?" If you are going to be non-compliant, don't live in the same neighborhood as your doctor.

We told a young man, who we anticipated would be noncompliant, "We will know if you have been walking on this cast."

He came in with duct tape on the bottom of the cast to hide that he had been walking on it.

We sometimes tell people that they can be TTWB (toe touch weight bearing). The next visit this kid comes in, no crutches, and walking on his toes!

The Honey-Do List

Adults, you would expect, will at least make an effort to do the right thing to get better. But, not always. I saw a thirty-year-old with an ankle fracture that I didn't think needed surgery in that moment, but it might, if it moved or changed. I like to check those fractures fairly soon so if it does shift, we can get it fixed in surgery before it is too far healed. The patient showed up five months later. It had obviously healed. Fortunately, in a satisfactory position. I asked him, "So, why didn't you come in sooner?" He said, "Well, I've been really busy. My wife's Honey Do list was so long, I didn't have time to come in. You see, she's really short, 5'2", and she can't reach anything."

"YOU WHAT?" Turns out he was in rehab for narcotics addiction.

Bad Prognostic Signs

'Prognosis' means the prediction of what's likely to happen. In medicine, we have what we call Bad Prognostic Indicators or Signs, which refers to something that shows up and you immediately think, "This is not going to go well." Skip Repass, one of our PA's (Physician's Assistant) and I kept a list of all the crazy things that showed up. Most of what follows comes from that list.

Bipolar Guy

Noncompliance can cause big problems. A guy came in with really bad arthritis in his ankle. It was end stage, bone on bone. There was nothing that would help, short of a surgical fusion. But I normally like to try conservative things first. He was adamant that he only wanted the surgery and as soon as possible. He had bipolar psychiatric disease, but seemed to have it under control with his medications. An older and wiser orthopaedic surgeon would have insisted on going ahead with the conservative treatment, even though it would have been ineffective. But I was neither older, nor wiser yet. So, I scheduled his surgery.

The case of Bipolar Guy was a nightmare from the very start. He went berserk in the hospital complaining of pain, but we could find no objective reasons for this and had to get a psych consult the first post op day.

On his first post op visit to the office, his splint was completely destroyed. This was the first bad prognostic sign. So I asked him, "How did that get so destroyed?" He said, "I was walking on it." "You were WHAT?" This was in spite of explicit instructions to be non-weight bearing. That was the second bad prognostic sign.

Every visit, it was something else that further compromised the surgery and the fusion disintegrated in a rapid fashion. That was the third bad prognostic sign. If he had been compliant, it could have been salvaged. He disappeared and about six months later we got a request from malpractice lawyers for the medical records. But even the personal injury sharks (oops- attorneys) would not actually take the case because I had so carefully documented all the noncompliance and explained all the repercussions.

Lesson learned. Who you operate on is just as (or maybe more) important than the pathology you are actually dealing with. That is, the "art" of medicine may be more important than your actual technical skill. It's a good idea to get to know the patient over a period of time before going straight into surgery for a non-urgent problem. You might get an inkling if there are any red flags you should pay attention to.

Seeing Patients in the Office

I am an orthopaedic surgeon. We operate. We fix things (we think). We heal with steel. A chance to cut is a chance to cure. But before we operate, we have to decide who to operate on. Except for the Emergency Room (ER), surgeries come from seeing patients in the office.

My schedule was divided up between the office and the OR. I spent seven half days (15-20 patients each) in the office and three half days in surgery doing six to eight surgeries a week. The math tells you that for every one patient I operate on, I must see eight to ten patients. So, we are really office doctors, who also operate. The decision to do surgery is covered in the next chapter. This chapter talks about our main patient interactions, which takes place in the office or clinic.

So, let's enter the world of "Seeing Patients." Patients can be mysterious, frustrating, astonishing, rewarding, certainly interesting, stressful, mind boggling, amusing, compelling, delightful, intriguing, memorable and sometimes tortuous.

For those of you who have done this, you have all experienced similar encounters. Enjoy the stories! Those of you who have not yet "seen patients" or never will, sit back and enjoy the ride. You may learn a few things.

Appointments

After all these years, how people get to us doctors individually is still somewhat of a mystery. When you first start, nobody knows you from Adam and people are put in with you primarily because they called the number for your group, hopefully because of their good reputation. Or, they are desperate and will take anybody who will see them. That reputation may be from years of good patient care (you hope), but may be because of slick advertising campaigns or the doctors are affiliated with some sports team. I was never good at self-marketing and didn't like that whole concept for medical care, dinosaur that I am.

After a while, people come in to see you through referrals from people who have already seen you. Word of mouth advertising is the best kind, I think. But that takes a while.

As I've already alluded to, appointments are a never ending stream of enigmas. I decided to specialize in knees and ankles. (One friend told me they tried to make an appointment to see me for their knee and they were not allowed because "Dr. Chase only sees people for problems between the knee and the ankle.")

When people come in for appointments, we give them lots of instructions. One of them is to turn off their cell phone so a ringing phone does not interrupt their visit with the doctor. One patient didn't show up for his pre-op appointment. This was very unusual because he was having surgery that week, which they usually don't forget. We called and called his cell phone. Voicemail. So we called his work. Not there. We called his wife and she said, "He is at his pre-op appointment." And indeed, he was! Sitting in our waiting room. He was completely forgotten about after he checked in and wasn't answering his cell phone because he had dutifully turned it off, as instructed. Not our best day!

Before You Walk Into the Room

Before you walk into the exam room, there can be some red lights that go off. Before you have even laid eyes on the patient, you know there's going to be trouble. The first thing I always did was review their chart and if they were new to me, review the medical records they brought in with them.

One principle I have learned over the years is this: the likelihood of a patient having significant pathology is inversely proportional to how many joints they complain about. In plain English, that just means, the more things they complain about, the less likely I am to find a real problem.

Electronic Medical Records

I am not a fan of electronic medical records (EMR's). To me, EMR's are like a nude beach. The idea of them sounds very appealing, but when you see what they are really like, it's pretty ugly! Dictations allow nuances of information that box clicks do not.

What to Call People

I had a peculiar way to figure out what name to call people when I walked in the room. If they were my age or younger (and by the end, that got to be most of the patients), I would call them by their first name. If they were ten or more years older than I am, I would address them as Mr., Mrs., or Ms. I felt this was a sign of respect. Anyone who fell within that ten-year gap in between, I would decide based upon how reasonable I thought they were during the visit. Anybody younger than me that I called Mr. or Mrs. became a code for me (and the staff and the therapists) to watch out! You can't get that information from clicked boxes.

Allergies

These are tough. Most things people write down as allergies are not. But, a real allergy can be life threatening, so you have to take all listed allergies seriously. There is no biological explanation that I know of, but I have noticed that the more allergies somebody has, the more of a "challenge" they will be. A nurse anesthetist I worked with had a formula for it: pre-op sedation = Versed .5 mg per allergy. (Okay, medical joke!)

Some of the allergies that patients have told us about include:

"I'm allergic to everything." (Really?)

"I am allergic to everything but Dilaudid." (This is a ploy to get a prescription for that very narcotic.)

"I'm allergic to Oxygen." "YOU WHAT?! What kind of reaction do you get to Oxygen?" "It makes my nose dry."

"My 12-year-old has an allergy to Cannabis." ("HE WHAT?" How did the parents know? Did the kid steal theirs? Are they giving it to him? Is he getting it on the street?)

Medical history

Bad Prognostic Signs to look for when you review the patient medical history include:

They refuse to fill out their medical history.

Their medical history has fibromyalgia, depression, anxiety, narcolepsy, migraines, PTSD and "Idiopathic Chronic Total Body Pain."

They have had ten back surgeries.

They forget (or don't bother) to check "yes" to their major medical problems.

They have 13 Workmen's Compensation claims and 6 liability claims.

Weight

In Orthopaedics, the patient's weight is a *Vital Sign*. The higher the weight, the more it stresses their bones and muscles and the more likely they are to break down. And, the higher their weight, the more trouble we have treating it and the more complications there are. It's just physics!

Before we call them back, we have an idea their weight might be high when the X-ray report says, "Moderate to severe burden of subcutaneous adipose tissue."

My assistant would then get their vital signs. My nurse Mary asked one patient, "How much do you weigh?" This was just for a ballpark to get the scale in the right general range. We always checked and got a real number. (People don't lie about their weight, do they?)

This particular patient said she weighed 235 pounds. Mary thought to herself, "No way!" Then she asked her to get on the scale. The actual number was 325 pounds! This patient had either major denial or a bad case of number dyslexia.

I had another patient who required a spinal needle to inject cortisone into their knee and hip. (A regular needle was too short.)

Sometimes patients would refuse to be weighed. Our response was, "This is important. We need it." There were various responses to that. Sometimes they would agree, but say "Don't tell my spouse how much it is." Sometimes they would agree, but say, "Don't tell me how much it is."

Another encounter went something like this:

"I'm not going to be weighed. I have OCD and I can't do it."

"They weighed you in the hospital."

"Well, I'm not doing it. Can I have some pain medicine?"

"We need your weight for that."

"Well, I won't be needing your services" was the response, as she stormed out of the room.

Other Before You Walk in the Room Warning Signs

Their pain diagram has tears streaming down the face.

They get into a fight with other people in the waiting room.

Your x-ray tech says, "Good luck," as you walk into the room.

Barbara Ann, my nurse at the time, walks out of the room, leans back against the wall, rolls her eyes back and says, "Aaaaaargh!!"

Going In

So, you walk into an examining room and you have no idea what you are going to encounter.

When there are kids, especially toddlers, in the office, it usually doesn't go well. They will melt down. That's what they do. When that happens, the parents can't pay attention to you when you are trying to talk to them because they are trying to prevent the child from eating the rubber gloves and dumping out the trash in the room. Try having the anterior cruciate ligament (ACL) discussion with a mom wrestling with two toddlers. Nothing will sink in!

Immediate Bad Prognostic Signs when you walk into the room:

They are crying as you walk in.

They take their Kleenex out of their right hand to shake your hand. (Gross!)

Both the patient and her daughter do this. (Double gross!)

Their cell phone rings while you are talking to them. They put up one finger and say, "Just a Minute. Let me take this."

They won't look you in the eye.

They wear slippers and/or pajamas to the office visit.

They have 30 bracelets on one wrist, 15 on the other and 30 rings.

They are wearing two inch heels while using a walker or cane for stability.

They have sunglasses on in the office.

A 70-year-old male is wearing a T-Shirt that says, "Sarcasm. It's better than killing people."

Tooth to tattoo ratio is less than one.

You walk into the room and are overpowered by the smell: perfume, dirt, body odor, alcohol, cigarette smoke, dead or rotten tissue, or wet skin under the cast.

They have an "emotional support" Chihuahua in a shoulder bag.

The Interview

It is said the most common interaction a surgeon has is the interview. It is done with every patient on every visit. So, you better learn how to talk to people. It is also said that a surgeon interrupts the patient he is talking to within 10-15 seconds after that interview begins. The reason a surgeon gets sued is usually not incompetence, it is a bad doctor-patient relationship that starts with the patient thinking, "That doctor didn't listen to me," (which he didn't). Research has shown that if the surgeon just bit his tongue for 60 seconds, only 60 seconds, (and often only 40 seconds), and didn't interrupt, that patient thought they were the most caring, listening, compassionate doctor the patient ever met, even if he wasn't.

History of Present Illness

Next comes talking, going through the history of the reason why they are there. I let them talk for that 60 seconds and it was amazing what came out of their mouths. Here are a few examples of how people described their pain:

"The pain is bad, but not so bad it is decapitating."

"Sometimes you feel pain where you think it is not."

"It's like putting a Band-Aid on a tidal wave."

"Is it better, worse or the same?" "None of those."

What is your level of pain? "Anything over a 10."

"My knee is weak, bubbly and prickly and it has vapors coming out of it."

"It doesn't hurt, but there is pain."

"My pain is in a smiley face pattern."

"My knee is disturbed."

"I feel like my blood is not working."

"I'm a knee person." (What does that mean?)

Other things they say:

"I'm a crier!"

"I'm a doctor's wife." (It's never good if they are starting with this. This is the medical version of DYKWIA-Do You Know Who I Am?)

"That other doctor is an asshole." (RED flags here. He might be, but this is not a good omen!)

"It really doesn't matter who I see. You were available first."

"I usually go to Dr. Smith, but he couldn't take me for three weeks." (The implication here is, "And I will never see you again after he is available.")

Beware of SomeDude! Everybody who has seen people with injuries has encountered this. When asked, "How did this happen?" The response is, "I was just mindin' my own business and SomeDude just came up and whacked me! I wasn't doin' *nuthin!!* He just came up, out of the blue, and he whacked me." SomeDude is everywhere. All over the country. And he has brothers. Big Dude, Little Dude, Bad Dude and, worst of all, Mean MF Dude! Watch out for them!

In response to, "Are you on any medications?" I once heard, "Sometimes I take my Mom's Blood Pressure medicines." In response to "What medicines are you taking?" I've heard, "I don't know. I drew pictures of my pills because I can't remember the names of them."

I had a patient who came in for his ankle and told me, "I went to a chiropractor."

"YOU DID WHAT? Why would you go to a chiropractor?"

He said, "My lawyer sent me."

(Lots of bad prognostic signs here.)

I asked, "Was it fractured?"

He said, "No, thank heaven. It was only broken." (That's much less serious.)

Then he said, "I'm having problems with my new brace."

I asked, "Well let's look at it."

He said, "I didn't bring it in."

("YOU WHAT?")

I asked another patient, "Does this keep you from doing anything?" He replied, "Only going to the mall!" (One of my all time favorites!)

Comments During Physical Exams:

"I'm a farter," (as you are examining their back.)

"I'm a fainter."

"Does it hurt here, here or here?" (Three places.) "Both."

"I need to listen to your heart."- "Can you hear it through these boobs?"

"Bend your knee." - "Which way?"

"Be careful, there might be some pee-pee down there," as I am looking at her ankle.

Antics, Faux Pas, and Aphorisms

One of my aphorisms is this: "The value of advice given is directly proportional to the intelligence of the person receiving it." And, there is no explaining some of the things people do and say.

I once asked a teenager to "Lie down flat on the bed." He proceeded to lay down perpendicular to the bed.

One time, while checking reflexes, I heard a loud 'clang' as their ankle monitor hit the metal support on the table. You learn not to ask.

Once, I was examining a patient's knee while sitting. I looked over to their midline and said, "What is that?" Then I realized it was their abdominal pannus. (Body Mass Index (BMI) was 67.6)

When I asked a young man why he lost his prescription for narcotics, he replied, "I don't do well with paper."

One woman asked me point blank, "Are you going to give me any pain medicines?"

I replied, "No ma'am."

She said, "Are there any doctors here who will give me pain medicines?"

I said, "I don't think so."

She said, "Well I am going to join a group and we are going to fight this."

More Patient Interactions

Sometimes patients just want to know that there is not something bad, awful or terrible happening to them and when they hear that, they relax visibly. Other times, patients just do and say things that defy explanation. Here are a few more interesting examples:

They want to get back to competitive tennis while on disability for fibromyalgia.

They are texting while I am talking with them.

They threaten to kill you if you don't give them pain pills.

She wants to be declared disabled so she can't fly home to work in snowy New York.

I once told an older man not to have a baker's cyst aspirated because it will recur. He came back after getting an aspiration elsewhere and said, "It's still there."

"Didn't I tell you that?"

"Yes, but the internet said it would go away. So I guess maybe that wasn't correct?" (Ah yes, the infallible internet!)

One of my biggest pet peeves is people who are noncompliant, but keep coming back complaining that they aren't getting better. I wonder why?

While patients can be interesting and even whacky, it's not all bad. One of my favorite requests was from a woman who said, "Can you give me a note that says my husband has to do whatever I tell him to do?"

The Ladies Call Me Billy

We see lots of patients. But some stand out. And a few are so memorable, they will never be forgotten. William, 25 years old, came in to see me about his knee. Warning lights started to go off quickly. Occupation listed on his form was "All around-esque work." (What is that?)

I entered the room and was blown over by the smell of cigarettes. He had a nice suit coat on and no underwear! (WHAT?) And, on his ankle was a police ankle monitor!! I like to find out what name patients' like to be called and I said, "Do you go by William or Bill or Will?"

He said, "The ladies call me Billy." (Uh-oh, that I didn't need to know.)

I then started the interview and he said, "My knee feels hollow." (What? I've never heard that before in 30 years of seeing patients.)

I asked, "When does your knee hurt the most?"

"When I am performing my manly responsibilities." (Oh Lord!)

What kind of work do you do?"

"I wait tables, but I am really an entrepreneur."

By now, I am quite skeptical of any answer. "How can you be an entrepreneur? You are only 25?" He replied, "I have one share of GE stock."

His mother, who was in the room, shook her head. Then he said, "Maybe I should get married."

My assistant, N'deevah, who by now was rolling with laughter, said "Maybe if you got a real job you could find a girl you would be proud to bring home to your mother here."

Doctors Too

It's not just the patients who can be a conundrum. One of my favorite people in the world, a great person and skilled spine surgeon, had a little problem with time management. My first week in practice, I had no surgeries of my own. So, Sylvia scheduled me to help Greg with two spine surgeries, each taking about an hour and a half. There was usually about an hour turnover between cases. We, of course, got a late start and were starting our second case about 11am.

Greg was on call and got a call from the emergency room (ER) to go reduce a wrist fracture, which would take about an hour. There was no way he was going to get to the office by 1PM, when he was scheduled to start seeing patients. I figured he would be lucky to get there by 3 or 3:30PM. He looked at the clock and said to the nurses, "Would you call the office and tell them I'm going to be about a half hour late?"

"HE WHAT? He said a half hour late?"

Running Late in the Office

You need a realistic idea of how long things will take. One of the big complaints we, and everybody else who sees patients, hear is "I didn't see the doctor until half an hour to an hour and a half after my appointment time." Legitimate complaint. We are awful. I was a little less awful because I hated to make people wait. But it still happened to me. I did everything I could to keep that to a minimum. I always started on time. If I was going to be late, (surgery, traffic, whatever) I would always call and have the office inform the patients and give them the option of rescheduling. But it inevitably happened. We (I) would get behind.

The best explanation I have heard for this was from Mike Mac-Millan, a fellow resident at the University of Florida and a close friend since the day we met in 1980. Mike is the king of analogies. His goes like this:

You walk into a grocery store behind several people and you all go get your groceries. When you get to the checkout line, some of those people have small baskets of groceries and don't take long to check out. Other people have these huge baskets of groceries. When you get in line behind several people with large baskets of groceries, you are going to wait. When you get in line behind other patients with large baskets of problems (complicated cases, millions of questions), you are going to wait!

There are a million reasons you can get behind. The worst is starting late. You can never catch up. Sometimes it's not preventable, but it usually is. I always left myself an hour to get stuff done before seeing patients and if I got delayed, it was just out of my time, not the patient's.

Another big reason we get behind is… Patients are late for their appointment! If you are late for your appointment, that makes everybody behind you late by that same amount of time - all day. You never catch up. (There is a theme here.)

The big dilemma is, do I see that patient who is late (10, 20, 30, 45 or infinite minutes late) and make all the people behind them (who were on time for their appointment) late? Or do I tell them, "You missed your appointment. You need to reschedule." Then, they are mad and trash you to everybody on the way out and to ten of their friends? You can't win. Somebody is always mad. How much time should you wait?

A patient has an emergency, real or perceived, and you work them in because that is part of your responsibility when you are treating patients. You get calls from the hospital about your patients. You have to answer those and sometimes, they're complicated. If you are on call for the emergency room, you have to take it and sometimes you have to leave. Part of the deal. But patients in the office waiting don't understand and they complain, even when it is explained to them.

Then there are unjustified reasons to make patients wait in the office. Calls about your personal business. People just stopping by the office just to say hi. (You don't want to be rude.) Reps wanting to detail you, and promote their product, while you make patients wait. Clinic business with your partners. Visiting with staff. Not to mention if you get upset about something (like when a patient dies, or has a big complication, or you have a confrontation with a patient and you can't get it out of your mind.)

Now that doesn't excuse the many anticipated delays, the most prominent being overscheduling. If you have patients scheduled every five to six minutes, with no regard for new vs. established (new always takes longer), you are going to get backed up. I came as close to anybody I know at staying on time. The patients appreciated it. I got lots of compliments about how close to their appointment people were seen. But it was at great expense to me, literally and figuratively.

If you are always running behind, I don't know how you handle that stress all the time. Some people aren't stressed about it at all and don't care if people are waiting for hours. Some, like me, get anxious due to their pathologic punctuality and are stressed all the time.

CHAPTER 4

PEOPLE SKILLS

Want to avoid those "YOU WHAT?" Moments? Developing your 'people skills' will go a long way toward a lasting, rewarding and fulfilling career.

Smile!

This simple act makes a huge difference. I learned this when I was in the hospital myself for major surgery and was pretty miserable. I was by myself when the cleaning lady came in. She had a big smile on her face and said, "How ya doin'?" I felt better, for no other reason than a smile!

I began to notice as I walked into a room, if the patient was smiling, I had an immediate good first impression. If they were cross or sullen with a frown, I picked up on that too and thought "Whoa, this could be trouble," even if it didn't actually turn out to be. The absence of a smile became a bad prognostic sign for me. Cranky people tend to be unhappy people. And unhappy people often create more to be unhappy about. Even if you don't feel like it, smile when you walk into a room and your patients will like you more. In fact, the whole visit will go better. Along with your smile, if you can get them to smile or laugh, they will feel the whole visit went better.

Use Humor Appropriately

I used to walk in and ask, "And this (person sitting with them) is your ...?" Primarily not to screw it up. But I would follow it up with, "I just didn't want to make any wrong assumptions." And they would laugh. Smile obtained.

I would often end a patient discharge with, "And you can stay away from orthopaedic surgeons. We are good people to stay away from." A laugh or a smile always helps.

But sometimes it can backfire on you. When transferring a patient from the stretcher to the operating table, the nurse said, as she had done dozens of times before, "Don't fall off the bed and onto the floor. We don't want to fill out all that paperwork!" Ha ha!

The patient replied, "My first wife fell off an operating table and had to go to the hospital." Uh oh! The silence was deafening. "Alright, let's go to sleep now." We had to hope that the Versed pre-op sedation kept him from remembering that little conversation.

Watch what you say and where you say it. Patients always think whatever is being said around them is about them. If you are laughing, they think you are laughing at them. Even if you do everything right, you can get in trouble. One patient, whose referring diagnosis was "radiculitis" (pain shooting down the leg from a pinched nerve above) came in and said, "That other doctor called me ridiculous!"

Learn to Read Body Language

I wish I had taken a course in nonverbal communication. Being able to read body language would have been a great help in dealing with patients. The amount of information you obtain "in the blink of an eye" when you first meet someone is both extensive and surprisingly accurate. A book written by Malcom Gladwell, *Blink,* talks about this. I know I have gotten much better at it over the years, just from experience. I learned when discussing various treatment options for a patient that if I could read what they were thinking, non-verbally, and recommend what they wanted, if appropriate, they thought I was a really good doctor! If their head was nodding up and down as I said, "I think we should try an injection before considering surgery," I knew I was on the right track.

But if I would have had some formal education or training in reading nonverbals, I believe it would have made a big difference in me figuring out what those real agendas were and I could have addressed them in better ways.

My kids used to say, "Dad, you are so judgmental!" Perhaps I was, but I had to be when I was at work. We sometimes had to make very rapid decisions with patients, especially during emergencies, and I had to be very judgmental fairly quickly. You might as well learn how to be a better judge.

Listen

It is important to listen to people. And you can't do it when you have patients scheduled every six minutes. It's what patients want and expect, but it can also keep you from getting sued. Research has shown that surgeons are notorious for interrupting patients after only ten seconds. As I said earlier, if they would just shut up and let the patient talk, uninterrupted, for 60, yes just 60 seconds (and maybe only 40), the patient would believe they were the most caring, compassionate doctor they had ever met. It also reduces medical negligence suits significantly.

The other time you need to listen is when a patient has a complication. There's a tendency to want to get away from them. They may remind you of a failure (not necessarily yours) that makes you feel bad and if you can get away, you won't feel so bad. But you need to spend more time with them, not less. It might keep them from seeking out an attorney for a malpractice claim. If you did nothing wrong, you might not lose the case (who knows in those things), but you will still have to go through it. It is very painful, let me assure you.

No VIP's

I don't believe in VIP's. I hated when office staff said, "We have a VIP coming in today." Nobody is more important than anybody else. There may be people who you might make accommodations for in scheduling because they have an important business relationship with your group. I get it. But I am not going to treat them any different than any other patient. That would mean I was doing something inadequate for everybody else I saw. I don't think that's a good idea. I want people to treat me exactly the way they treat everybody else. When you start doing things differently from the way you always do it, that's when things go wrong.

Be Humble

Be humble because the minute you get full of yourself and you think you are God's gift to the operating room, you will be humbled. I try not to take too much credit when things go well. Then, I don't have to take all the blame when they don't.

Handling Complications

As a surgeon, you better be able to handle a complication. Because you will get them (unless of course you are perfect and never have any). You have to get ready for those complications that are totally unexpected and are nobody's fault. The proverbial "one of those things." You feel bad for the patient, but you know you didn't cause it. We would like to be able to identify why something happens, but you can't always. Stuff Happens!

Then there are those that are clearly your fault. You screwed up. You forgot something, got distracted, or slipped in the OR. The patient may or may not have been hurt by it. Or, it can be devastating, especially if there are long term bad effects for the patient.

The most common circumstance will be something bad happened and your guilt kicks in. You question, "What did I do wrong?" even if you didn't do anything wrong. We all take these things very personally and it haunts us. We absolutely take it home, often to the detriment of our family who may have no idea why Dad is in such a bad mood or why he yelled at me. Handling complications well is an important skill to develop.

Be Honest and Straightforward

If you tell somebody you are going to do something, then do it. Don't tell the OR you will be there in 20 minutes when you know it will be 40. Don't schedule a case for an hour when you know it will take an hour and a half. Don't abuse "stat." Almost nothing in orthopaedics is stat.

If a patient has a difficult problem that won't get better, tell them that, even though they may not want to hear it. Look them in the eye. Sometimes it is easier (and quicker, especially if you are two hours behind) to give them a rosy picture. It cuts down on a lot of questions. People want to be leveled with. It gives them realistic information so they can make plans. Don't give them false hope. You don't have to be the picture of doom and gloom, but level with them. If you are not honest, you will lose your credibility. There are not a whole lot of things more important than that.

Names

Names are important. My wife tells me I have a gift. I can remember names. Patients, staff, friends and acquaintances from the past. I am very lucky. At my retirement party at the surgery center, the repeated comment I got on the cards written by the nurses was how much they appreciated me remembering their names. It's important to people. You don't have to use it every other sentence, like a used car salesman. But just let them know that you know who they are. We all have different skills. If you're not good at remembering names, use technology or some kind of mnemonic devices to help.

Treat People Decently

Remember the basics. Say please and thank you. The people you are working with are not trying to sabotage you. They are usually doing their best. It helps nothing to yell. The squeaky wheel does indeed get the grease, but if you weren't so mean, people might go out of their way to help so you don't have to make so much noise.

I remember hearing in the OR "Can anybody stay for an add on case for Dr. Smith?" The staff would all say, "Dr. Smith? Nope. I have an appointment I have to get to." Dr. Smith is well known for yelling at the staff. It is very counterproductive. You make everybody tense, they overthink and then screw up (maybe) and then there's more yelling. It just compounds itself. If the same request was for Dr. Jones (who is very nice to the staff), the answers would be very different. "Sure! I'd be happy to." Being decent is just the right thing to do.

My Favorite Part: Taking Care of Nice People

The office can be fun if you have enough time to give to people and are not stressed out of your gourd because you are two hours behind. Many orthopaedic injuries or surgeries can take months to get over, and often years, if you are following them for a chronic problem. So you get to know the patients. In some cases, that is not pleasant. In others, it is rewarding and fulfilling.

My favorite part of what I do (or did) is taking care of nice people! Sometimes people, out of the blue, tell you how pleased or impressed they are with what you did and how grateful they are, even if you didn't do anything extraordinary or sometimes anything at all.

Sometimes a patient who you think did terribly winds up sending people to you. "THEY WHAT?" And you think "Why?" Probably because you just listened to them, which is what they needed the most. But that doesn't happen if you don't have the time.

The crazy stories that fill this book are actually the rare ones (usually). They stick out because they are memorable. And, they are often attached to strong emotion! In a strange way, the really nice people who do well are not the ones that stand out, even though they are exceedingly more common than the chronically unhappy.

I have been blessed to make connections with some really nice people. And over the years, some have become friends.

In addition to friends, some of the best professionals I have met have been my patients: Handyman, cabinet builders, cleaning ladies, roofers, veterinarians and more. For obvious reasons, I do wait until they are doing well and I am done treating them.

Treating Neighbors and Friends

This is tricky. Never treat family. You can't be objective. It clouds your judgement. Your friends want you to treat them because they like you and have confidence in you. That's what you want all your patients to feel like. BUT- your judgement can be clouded. Sometimes, you are just too close to them to make objective decisions. And it puts great pressure on you. What if things don't go well, through no fault of your own? It makes all interactions in the future, both in office and out, very sticky and awkward. When I got more confident after practicing for a few years, I would do friend's surgeries, but only if it was something I did all the time and risks were low. I did refer some people to my partners, just because they were too close. That is a tough judgement call. There is no easy answer.

Getting the Best Information

It is important to get all the best and most accurate information you can about your patient. It helps you make the right decision about your recommendations for them. These are a few things you do NOT want to hear in pre-op:

"I'm having surgery for my third AAA in January." (AAA is an aneurysm or weakness in the artery wall that can burst if there is too much fluctuation in blood pressure, which can happen in surgery.)

"You didn't write that down."

"There wasn't a box for it."

One time, I heard, "I should probably get my transfusion first before the surgery."

"TRANSFUSION? "For WHAT? There is nothing in your medical history."

"Sorry, I forgot"

"YOU FORGOT?"

It is important to know if someone is getting regular blood transfusions.

Another time, I walked into the pre-op area and the patient's mother, who I hadn't met yet, said, "Do you need to know that all her brothers and sisters have to get an injection before any surgeries?"

"THEY WHAT? For what?" It turned out, they all had an inherited clotting defect. That surgery went fine with the right injection before surgery. Without it, they can bleed uncontrollably! But the patient didn't say anything and it was nowhere in the medical records. Catastrophe averted, by pure dumb luck. That is not how we like to find out about those things.

Questions You Don't Want to Ask

A general principle is, don't ask questions you don't want to know the answer to.

"What does that tattoo say?" (Or mean is even worse.)

"Why do you have so many tattoos?"

"Why are you wearing that ankle monitor?"

"When are you due?"

"Is this your mother?" I did this in the pre-op area. Answer was, "No, it's my wife!" You can't dig yourself out of that hole.

Review the chart

I remember very vividly when I was in high school and how distressed my dad (who was not medical) was when he came back from taking my grandmother to her first post-op appointment after a brain biopsy. He said, "The neurosurgeon started talking to us and none of it made any sense. He suddenly got up, left the room, and came back and said "Heh, heh, I'm sorry. I got you mixed up with somebody else."

"YOU WHAT?" (It's not just patients who do YOU WHAT? moments.)

It can happen. We can't remember everything. That is what charts are for. But take a minute to look at it before you go in. It might be just laziness - or wait – maybe you're in too much of a rush because you are overbooked?

Incentive

"Why would anybody not want to get better?" Welcome to the world of perverse disincentives to get better or what is called "secondary gain."

The classic examples are patients with a Worker' Compensation injury (they get paid 60% of their wages if they are not working) and litigation (if they get better, their case goes away and they and their lawyer don't get any money.) The worst of all is when they have both!! We have an old saying "Your lawyer does not want you to get better."

Hovering Family

Another Bad Prognostic Sign is hovering family, and lots of them. When there are more people in the room than chairs, it is not a good sign. But the most ominous sign is when whoever is there with them is rubbing their shoulders, cooing "It will be alright" as you are talking to them. This is classic for enablers and you can be quite suspicious that the patient will not take much responsibility or make much effort to get better. Secondary gain, again. "I lose all this attention if this gets better." They may not be consciously thinking that, but subconsciously, they are.

A patient of mine came in and wouldn't bend her knee past 30 degrees. It must be locked, I thought. But her sugar daddy was rubbing her shoulders. Bad sign. Magnetic resonance imaging (MRI) showed nothing. Because she couldn't bend it, maybe something was blocking it so we did an arthroscopy. Immediately under anesthesia, she could easily bend her knee to 130 degrees and nothing blocked the knee on the scope. Uh oh! Guess what? After months of therapy, she still wouldn't bend it past 90 degrees. Predicted bad result, with no objective pathology. I tell you, watch out for rubbing shoulders!

Observe When They Are Not Looking

You can get a lot of information by casually observing patient behavior when they don't think you are watching. Look out the window after their visit is over and if the terrible limp that was there in the office is now gone, their complaints may not be real or valid.

One obvious faker started to writhe around in pain when I asked him to bend his knee past 90 degrees while lying down (supine). Then, he sat up with his legs hanging at 90 degrees with no apparent pain whatsoever. There are protocols for figuring out if people are malingering, which just means, faking symptoms. Symptom magnification is a very real problem for us to sort out. And it is amazing how many people get better when their lawsuit for pain and suffering is over.

Gathering information is a critical step in treating patients. It's important to get good information because it can actually save their life. But it's also important to figure out if there are any ulterior motives or secondary gain issues. This brings us to our next topic, which is all about making decisions with patients.

CHAPTER 5
MAKING DECISIONS WITH PATIENTS

Your Patients Matter

Now that you have spent the time interviewing and examining the patient, let's talk about how you make decisions and recommendations for the problem they have.

Emergencies

Doctors have to make lots of decisions. Surgeons make lots of urgent decisions.

The first thing to figure out is if they have an emergency. There are not a lot of real emergencies in orthopaedics. But if there is, it means you deal with it now! If it's not, then it is what I call an "emergency of convenience," which is most of what we deal with. We might even say, "This needs to be taken care of in the next two to three days to one to two weeks." Orthopaedists are frequently adding on surgeries (we call them cases) to take care of those semi-emergencies.

Diagnosis

The next decision is, "What is the problem?" Sometimes that is an easy decision, or so it seems. One Friday night, I was covering the final football game for the high school where I am team doctor. There was only 30 seconds left in the game, so I said goodbye to the trainers and started walking to my car. Suddenly, I heard a collective "gasp" from the stands and turned around to see the trainers frantically waving their arms for me to get back there and out onto the middle of the field. When I arrived, I could see the obvious problem, a dislocated ankle. His leg was pointing north and his foot was pointing east, 90 degrees off.

Impressive! This young man was writhing around yelling about his knee hurting. I thought to myself, "You dummy, that is your ankle." I said, "Let's get you to the side and see if we can get that back in place." The ambulance was right there, so we got him in it and I tried to reduce the ankle (put it back in its proper place). After a couple of unsuccessful tries (Yes it did hurt!) I said, "We need to get you to the OR and take care of this under anesthesia."

When I met him in the ER, he kept yelling about his knee so I said, "Okay, let me look at your knee." As I start to look at the knee on the side of the ankle dislocation he says, "No, it's the other knee." "YOUR WHAT?" And he says "It's the other one. My ankle hardly hurts."

An x-ray of the left ankle showed the expected fracture dislocation. But the right knee showed a growth plate fracture completely displaced into the joint itself causing excruciating pain if he (or I, or anybody) tried to straighten his knee out. Then, I had to say to myself, "You dumb ass! That's the first thing you learn as in intern in the ER is to not focus on the most obvious injury, but do a thorough evaluation before making any decisions." Four hours later, after I had to fix both joints (now 5 am), I was still beating myself up for the rookie error. (To follow up, he did heal and actually played college football for a year.)

Sometimes, the diagnosis is fairly straightforward and you go about making the decisions around how to treat it. Sometimes, it's confusing and you are not sure exactly what it is that the patient has. Sometimes you have no earthly idea what is going on! This is when you start to sweat. "How am I supposed to tell them what to do when I have no idea at all what they have?"

This is when you start ordering tests. Appropriate to do, but you are also stalling for time. Sometimes, after much thought, later that day or in the car on the way home, it comes to you. Sometimes the gears just have to fall into place and mesh. Sometimes, even after ordering those tests, you still don't know what they have. What I learned to do was tell the patient, "You don't have anything bad, awful or terrible. I don't know what exactly you have, but I know what it isn't. Sometimes these things just evolve to the point where they are more obvious, so let's have you come back in one to three months to reassess." Most people are fine with that. Some are not, so they leave and tell everyone they know how bad a doctor that Dr. Chase is.

Sometimes you just never do know exactly what they had or have. What you have to learn is how to not give yourself an ulcer or heart attack beating your head against the wall. Do the best you can and leave it at the office. Easy to say. Sometimes very hard to do. You owe it to your family to learn this skill.

There will be people who are unhappy with your decisions, particularly if you can't identify a specific diagnosis. Be prepared. You would think it would be the opposite. "Great there is nothing wrong." But that's not usually the case. They have pain (real or imagined) and are upset there is no confirmation or that their secondary gain won't be met.

Is There a Problem?

Even if you are confident you have made a good diagnosis, the next decision is: "Is there a real problem here or are they the proverbial "Worried Well?" A significant number of people come in to make sure there is nothing really wrong and don't want a diagnosis.

How to Present the Problem

You try to make decisions based on science; the books we learned from and the journal articles we read. But sometimes there is conflicting information that tells you to do two exact opposite things. Another old saying: "There is lots of dogma, it's just all different." We are all products of our experience, sometimes despite what dogma or articles say.

"Good judgement comes from experience. Experience comes from bad judgement." That's a great quote from a great teacher, Dempsey Springfield.

A line I learned to use that was very helpful was, "If you do this will it hurt?" Yes. "Will it damage It?" No.

Be Conservative

Once you have a good diagnosis, then you have to decide what to do. Sometimes doing nothing is a good option or even the best option. A good old saying is, "Is the treatment worse than the disease? Is the problem fixable or are you just trying to make it not as bad?" We, as orthopaedic surgeons, have the option of offering people a surgical option. Pretty cool! My good friend Mike MacMillan once said, "There will always be a tiny Dempsey Springfield on our shoulders saying, "Are you sure you want to do that?" My general principal was always "Be conservative." If they have a complication, I want them to be absolutely sure they felt they really wanted to go ahead with the surgery and not because I talked them into it.

A number of aphorisms passed down to me by my faculty in residency (Dempsey Springfield and others):

1. You should do all you can to avoid an operation.

2. You should look for ways not to operate on somebody.

3. You can always operate. You can't un-operate.

4. If you are destined to have a bad result, it is better to have it non-operatively.

5. You operate on them, you own them.

Good lines I used to help patients choose surgery or no surgery:

"Your knee will tell you what to do and how bad it is will tell you when."

"Don't schedule surgery on this until the thought of living with it, as is, bothers you more than having that big operation I described."

You don't want to get the reputation of a "knife happy" surgeon. Get that and it is very hard to eliminate. It's a small world out there and once people start talking, you never know how many people they tell, "Don't go to Dr. Chase. He will always recommend surgery." Unless it is urgent, you lose nothing but a little time (mostly theirs) if you "sit on it and watch it." You want people to be confident that if you recommend an operation for them, that is the right thing to do, not just to line your pockets. Your good reputation is gained with much difficulty and lost in a heartbeat.

One of my basic principles of personal finances is: "Don't make financial commitments that require ever escalating income." What does this have to do with making decisions about surgery? You never want to be sitting in a room, looking at a patient and thinking, "Maybe I can extend the indications for this surgery a little. I have a big boat payment coming up soon."

Sometimes you have to make a decision that day about whether or not to do a surgery that is already scheduled. The patient has a scab in the operative site (risk of infection) or a cold (they could get complications from the anesthesia.) Should you cancel the surgery? Pain in the ass for you and them. What I would tell them was, "In a year, you and I won't remember we postponed this for a few weeks. If you have a complication from pressing ahead today on this elective operation, we certainly will."

And sometimes being conservative is not what the patient wants. Then they leave and tell everyone they know that you won't operate on them and you are not a very good doctor. Sometimes you can't win.

Surgical Options

Doctors are like point guards or quarterbacks. Their success is dependent on decisions they make. Once you and the patient decide that surgery is what they want to do for the problem, then you must decide what kind of surgery you are going to recommend. This is a discussion you (usually) have in your own head.

Sometimes, but not frequently, you talk to them about several surgical options. This can be a Pandora's box. The intricacies of each procedure are often (not always) way beyond what your average patient wants to get into. Of the various surgical choices, which do you recommend? Another great old saying: "The more surgical options for a problem are available, the less likely any one of them is a really good option."

Then you have to ask yourself, "Is this surgery I have proposed in my wheelhouse or should I refer it on?" Do you offer them the simpler option that you do or send them on for the more complicated option that you don't do? And if you recommend that simpler option, is it because you can do this one and can't do the other one? Here is where greed and/or ego can pop in. We all want to look competent in our patients' eyes, but don't bite off more than you can chew.

Be Honest

You want to be honest with your patients. That goes without saying. But obtaining *Voluntary Informed Consent* - the hallmark of obtaining permission to do the surgery - can be deceiving. You can make something innocuous sound like a death sentence and they will refuse the treatment. Or you can minimize even significant risks so it doesn't sound too bad and they go ahead.

Deciding on Surgery

You would like to think that all your patients are motivated, good solid citizens that want to get better and will work hard in therapy to accomplish that. Nope. Not even close. You have to take into account all factors that could affect the outcome. You might make entirely different decisions for two people with the exact same orthopaedic pathology, based upon their personality and life situations.

Some people are just not good operative candidates. Crazy is crazy. You can't fix crazy. But sometimes even crazy people really do have something wrong with them. Which creates a dilemma.

What to do with crazy patients with real pathology:

1. Emergency: No choice.

2. Symptoms fit objective pathology: Probably go ahead, with trepidation.

3. Symptoms are not consistent or nebulous, but they seem to be decent people: These are the hardest ones; depends on how everything fits.

4. Things don't fit: No.

5. A real jerk: Hell no!

One more bad prognostic sign is when a patient complains about their last doctor. A patient came in with a BMI of 55. When I asked why the previous doctor wouldn't do surgery, she said, "He said I was too fat!" Silence ensued. Finally, I had to think, "Yup, he was right." When talking about the other doctor, the patient said, "That doctor was an asshole!" Maybe he was, but I told myself, this is the end for you and me. If you are saying this about that doctor, what will you say about me?

When you make the decision to do surgery, you open yourself up to misery, if and when they don't do well. It can be difficult to balance the few saves with all that misery you will feel. Do you get to say, "I'm not going to operate on this person because I don't like them or I have a bad feeling?" That's a tough one.

Sometimes you go ahead and they fly through it and have no problem and you say "What was I worried about?" And some-times they do terribly, as you suspected, and you say, "Why did I do that?" And you are miserable. Every time you see them on the schedule you say, "Oh crap" and "I am never doing that again."

Dilemma: Exploratory Surgery

Sometimes you are put in a position of deciding whether to do "exploratory surgery." In Orthopaedics, this is not very common. We have good diagnostic tests that tell us what we are dealing with most of the time. And when the study doesn't show anything specific, we are fairly safe in saying, "You don't need surgery."

But sometimes you get the feeling that there really is something there. Do you operate? And is it exploratory surgery? By definition, you don't know what you will find. If they go ahead and they are not better, you better have said it was "exploratory" multiple times and documented it in the chart. If they are better, why? Was their pain from one of those things you trimmed away or did you get lucky or was it the placebo effect?

Set Realistic Expectations

Sometimes you do elective surgery on someone and they have bad results with no logical explanation. There is not a lot worse than having a patient say, "If I had known this, I would have never had this surgery." And everything seemed to fit. Neither you nor they did anything wrong. It's the proverbial "One of those things." But the truth is, you don't know beforehand. If you had that crystal ball, neither of you would have made the decision to have that surgery. This is why you don't promise great results, even though that is what the patient wants to hear. This is why you don't promise that "Everything will be fine' or "You'll do great". You don't know that. If you were a braggart before surgery, it will be very hard to deal with these people. You will be miserable. If you were humble, they might be more understanding.

Long Term Results Count

You will get patients who come in and want the latest and greatest thing they read about in a magazine on the plane or a friend told them about this new procedure or technique. You will have reps for the equipment and drug companies call on you and try to convince you to use their "Wonder drug" or "Foolproof prosthesis." Or, patients want this new minimal incision surgery or the replacement from the side. Don't fall for it. There is an old saying, "New and approved is not necessarily new and improved." What counts is long term results, documented by physicians who do quality science and long term follow up.

Insightful Stories

Vioxx was a wonder drug for inflammation. I used it personally and thought it was great. But reports began to filter in about cardiovascular side effects. So, I asked the Vioxx rep and they said, "We haven't heard anything about it." The next week, it was yanked from the market. Either the rep was lying through their teeth to me or they hadn't been given the information from their higher ups. Lesson learned. You can't believe anything from somebody who stands to profit from selling you that product. (You may say, "Then shouldn't it be the same for surgeons recommending an operation?" Good point. This is where patients have to hope that they are dealing with a professional, rather than a salesman.)

There's a story from my residency faculty, Dempsey Springfield, about a renowned hip surgeon who developed a new operation for aseptic necrosis of the hip, the Conservative Hip Replacement. It was a great idea. There was sound science and good early results. Then, almost like clockwork, three years after the surgery, patients started coming in with this new prosthesis failing due to loss of circulation to the top of the femur. The law of unintended consequences kicked in. It was consistent. How would you like to wake up every day and know that when you went into work, you were going to see three to four of your old patients with a collapsing hip that you invented and inserted at surgery?!

The point is not to never do anything new. The point is, let the scientists who are geared up to review their cases at five to ten years and report their results in peer reviewed journals inform you how those long-term results are turning out. Do something new when it solves a problem you are having, not just because it is new.

Humorous Stories

These stories shouldn't be funny, but they are.

A very obese man was in a doctor's office for lower spine pain. The doctor walks into the room, looks over his reading glasses at the patient, looks at the chart and then back at the patient. The first thing out of his mouth was, "Well, let's see if we can figure out why you have back pain."

A doctor walks into the room and puts up the x-ray on the x-ray board (yes that's how we used to do it before the picture archiving and communication system (PACS) on the computer) and says, "Wow, I've always wanted to do one of these operations."

Complications

If you operate, you will have complications. Count on it! You are deluding yourself if you think you won't. Even if you do everything perfectly, there will be people who don't do well. Objective complications are difficult to deal with, but at least there is an explanation. But the worst are subjective complaints, usually pain, without you being able to identify any reason for it.

As I mentioned before, you operate on them, you own them. Of course, their continued complaints are *solely* due to the operation you performed, not the natural course of the disease the patient (and now you) are dealing with. But even so, you feel responsible. When you operate on people, you take it very personally. "What did I do wrong to make this happen?" It's only natural. Doctors are generally very good at taking responsibility for things, even when it's not their fault. Some are not, but generally if you got here, you are a responsible person.

When you decide to operate, you are subjecting yourself to that possibility. And it can be miserable. It ruins your day when these people come in, not to mention theirs. That is why, as I got farther along in my career, my motto became: "My main goal with my surgery is to avoid complications, not make great saves." Younger surgeons are usually more willing to take those risks. Remember the old saying, "Maturity is when wisdom overtakes testosterone."

You will make decisions that will not turn out well and have complications. Any complication is hard to handle, but the more severe the complication (loss of limb, death, and other really bad ones), the more anguish you will go through. You better be able to handle it.

Your Good Name = Your Credibility

Sometimes people ask you to do something that is just plain wrong. Easy. Don't. Frequently they are "just trying to get something." Handicap parking stickers. Home health aide. Home physical therapy (PT). Motorized wheelchairs. Narcotics. You don't think it is needed, but sometimes you just feel like signing it to get them out of your hair and avoid the confrontation. Don't let the patient talk you into doing something. If you say something is "medically necessary" and it's not, you have started down that slippery slope. It gets easier and easier. Then you find you are doing it all the time. Now your word is suspect. There is nothing so important as your good word or good name.

Call Decisions

Some of the more difficult decisions you will make will be made in the ER. Difficult problems (horrible fractures, dislocations, limbs without circulation, etc.). Difficult patients. Just remember: do the right thing and you will sleep better. I'm not saying I always did. I laid in bed many nights after a call from ER and couldn't go back to sleep wondering if I should have done something different. Most times I was right, and sometimes wrong. I always felt better that I went in, even though I was more tired the next day and it was torture.

Discussing Errors

Have you ever made a mistake? Sure, you have. Everybody has. But doctors can't. Ever. Of course, I am being facetious. But you get my point. You "make a mistake" and there is a personal injury attorney "ready to demand justice," which coincides with filling his pocket with 40% of all proceeds from a suit or a settlement. For a doctor, that makes admitting to a mistake a terrifying proposition. If I admit to a mistake or actually bring it up, even if it is not evident, am I asking to be sued? Difficult ethical problem. But if there is an unforeseen event, you have to talk with the patient about it. Those conversations are not easy, but somewhat straightforward.

What's harder is when you or your team made a mistake and there is no apparent evidence that it caused any harm. (You gave one Tylenol tablet rather than the two they were supposed to get.) Or you slipped in surgery and the instrument went plunging but no apparent problem.

Do you bring that up? Dunno! Another difficult ethical problem. And I don't have the answers for all these problems.

Gifts from Patients

What's the problem here? Somebody wants to thank you and brings in something to give you. People are bringing in cookies or brownies or something like that all the time. No big deal. (Old saying: "If you eat something a patient brought in, ask if they were a happy patient first.") But it gets sticky as the gifts get bigger and more involved. Sleeve of golf balls? Probably okay. A dozen ProV1 golf balls, expensive bottles of wine, paintings, gifts for your kids? I've had all these. They can put you in a somewhat precarious position ethically, particularly when the giver makes a request later for something that may or may not be justified like a permanent handicap parking sticker or a special brace that may not be indicated, but the insurance will pay for it if you say it is "medically necessary". They don't even have to say anything. You and the patient both know what they gave you. The safest policy is to never take any gifts from patients. But are you going to be a jerk and say you won't take it when the little old lady brings in a plate of homemade chocolate chip cookies for the office to thank you for all the great work you all have done?

CHAPTER 6
THE OPERATING ROOM

The Culture of the OR

An orthopaedic surgeon I ran into years ago had recently retired and said he didn't miss much. (Me too.) But he did miss the "camaraderie of the operating room." (Me too.) I considered the people I worked with in the ORs some of the finest people I have had the pleasure to get to know. They had difficult hours and sometimes very demanding conditions to work in, with all the "challenging" surgeons they had to deal with. They were almost always unfailingly pleasant and if you weren't terrible to them, as helpful and respectful as they could be.

These people worked very hard with high stress from just being in surgery (the surgery itself or from the surgeons). People who work in the OR get very little thanks and lots of grief.

Surgeons get the pleasure of accomplishing something useful and working with people we like, usually.

Camaraderie

We rotate with different people in our room each day (unless of course you think you are so important that only very few staff are good enough for you). So, you get to know, pretty well, a number of different people. This group includes the orderlies, certified registered nurse anesthetists (CRNAs) and anesthesiologists. I always said, people in the OR know the real you better than anyone else in the world, except maybe your spouse. And sometimes they know facets of you even your wife doesn't.

They are with you for hours, sometimes under highly stressful times. And sometimes with no stress at all, just simple cases, prepping, closing, getting patients out of the room. We often tell stories; funny ones, serious ones, medical, non-medical or about our kids. I think that the quality of the experience for the staff was highly dependent on the atmosphere that the surgeon created in the room. You don't have to be as formal. The patient is asleep and, as soon as that happens, the solemnity eases. We don't stop being professional in what we are doing (paying attention to the details that need attention). Those conversations stop when the actual surgery is occurring. Everybody knows it.

It's interesting that the patients get good exposure to the people in the check-in area, the pre-op area and the recovery room. Their view of their experience is dependent on these groups of people, which is very important! But they don't get any exposure that they remember (because of medication or they are under anesthesia) to the people who take care of them in surgery itself.

Speaking of stories, the story of the Camouflage Butt Warmer is one of my favorites.

We discussed many things in the OR. One time, I was commenting on how bad a gift giver I was and our CRNA said, "It's not that hard. You listen to what your spouse is saying, what's important to her and tailor your gift to what her wishes are." "Good idea," I said. This was in the winter in Florida when my daughter Anna's high school soccer games were being played. No snow, but still really cold with the humidity. My wife was always miserable with the cold. I thought, "That's it. I'll get her something to keep her warm during those soccer games."

One night at the game, I noticed one of the Dad's picked up this pad he sat on, so I asked him what it was. He said "It's a microwavable seat cushion you heat up before you come to the game and it keeps you warm for hours." "Perfect," was my thought.

I should have known that my plan had some flaws when I was going to Bass Pro Shop to get my Wife's Christmas gift. Nor did I pick up on the clue that the only color it came in was camouflage.

Christmas day came and I was very proud of my gift. It showed I listened to my wife and took her needs and wants into consideration. When she opened it you could have heard a fishing hook drop! My oldest daughter, Megan, shouted "Dad, you are pathetic!!" Of course, my reply was "WHAT?" Now there is fear and trepidation in our house every Christmas over "What is Dad going to get Mom this year?"

ORs are Not Interchangeable

Occasionally you will hear politicians or administrators or insurance people say, "Just have the doctor go over to the other hospital and do some surgeries." Bad idea. You get used to people, they get used to you. The equipment is different. The staff know what you like and can anticipate what you need. There is nothing worse than saying, "I need this special instrument to finish this case." Only to hear, "We don't have it." "Shit!" So you either finish sub-optimally. (That's not what you or the patient wants, nor do you want to send to the other OR across town and leave the patient asleep for an extra one to two hours doing nothing but waiting. Awful.

Surgeons and Doctors

You think WHAT? You think surgery is fun? You are cutting people open. How can that be fun?

Medical Student Advice

I was faculty on clinical rotations for Florida State University School of Medicine students on their junior surgery rotations. A frequent conversation was about what specialty to go into. I heard students for years, especially when I was in residency, say "I really like surgery and would like to do it, but I just don't think I can get through the residency. I don't want to work that hard." This was said with good reason. It can be brutal.

I would tell them "This is a fork in the road. Only pick a surgical field if you just "have to do surgery." Not just that you would like to. You have to. If not, go into a nonsurgical field." It's too demanding (time, effort, the call, the responsibilities, the crap, the stress.) If you aren't really fulfilled by it, don't do it. That's a pretty good summary.

Difference Between Surgeons and Other Doctors

Surgeons have to be a little (sometimes a lot) egotistical, confident, maybe domineering. Some are self-centered or narcissistic. Mostly, they must be willing to make decisions decisively. You can't be wishy washy, (especially in the operating room). They usually like to be in control, which you are in the OR. You can see those traits in non-surgeons. But you usually don't see surgeons without them. The kicker is, you don't have to be an asshole. Your control in the OR is unassailable. You are in charge. The decisions made in the OR are not democratic. This is a large amount of power. With it comes almost total responsibility.

An old joke: A surgeon and an internist are running to catch an elevator. The internist sticks out his hands to stop the door from closing. You put out what you don't use. The surgeon sticks his head in the door to keep it from closing.

Doing Something

I chose surgery because you are actually doing something. You are intervening, changing things, fixing them, hopefully. Now, some things can't be fixed. I realize that. But you think you can fix it, or at least think you can help. Orthopaedics is a lot of that. Find a specific problem, address it, fix it, they get better (or they don't) and they go away (or they don't). Very episodic. You don't usually have the long-term relationship with patients after injuries heal like you do as a primary care doctor. That may be good. Surgeons are not necessarily personable, affable, pleasant, or gregarious enough to do that or they don't want to do that. But sometimes you do form those relationships. Certain problems (degenerative problems like arthritis) and certain people you just make a connection with and you can develop a long-term relationship.

Surgery Is in the Head, Not in the Hands

People talk about a surgeon's "good hands" and definitely that is true. Some people are proficient and skillful, and some are not. Just like any athlete. Some are just plain clumsy and they either get better or they don't last long. This you hear from the OR staff pretty quickly. Young surgeons are notoriously slower, but normally pick up as time progresses and they get more confidence. Dr. William F. Enneking, a nationally and internationally renowned orthopaedic surgeon at the University of Florida used to say, "Speed is an accomplishment, not a goal." But doing the actual surgery is mental. Your hand just follows what your brain tells it to do. (Duh!)

That involves experience. If you don't have the experience, prepare. Review the anatomy and review the technical steps of the procedure. If that is not clear in your mind, you are going to dawdle. If you know where the important things are, be careful when you are in the vicinity of those structures, then you can proceed with dispatch.

That 'doing something' presents an inherent conflict of interest. Fee for service rewards volume and the ultimate volume is surgery. Procedures are reimbursed way better than "cognitive services." It's the way it is. Should you get more for taking the risks of doing surgery? I think so. (I'm a surgeon.) But that doesn't mean cognitive services should be so poorly rewarded.

This can pose an enormous risk for patients if their surgeon is recommending surgery for reasons other than their best interest. In all the years I did this, I saw a few surgeons who recommended surgery to nearly everybody they saw. (Aggressive indications?) Did they do it because they believed in it? Maybe. Because they made more money? In some cases.

What I saw most frequently was not surgeons doing unindicated things. They would just see volumes of patients and even with reasonable indications they would get lots more surgery (and lots more money) just because of volume.

There are reasonable differences, in my opinion, about indications for surgery. Some surgeons are very aggressive and perfectly justified by the literature. Others, such as me, were much more conservative. So, I would see very busy surgeons making big money and not be unethical at all. Just busy. Really busy.

Doing Surgery

There is stress in surgery, no doubt. But for most elective cases where there is a good workup, you don't get too many surprises. If the case is routine, no problem. If it is not, then you prepare. Review the anatomy, the procedure, and how the equipment works. That is 90% of your time.

The stress comes in emergency cases where you don't have that time to review. You go directly from blissful ignorance at home, to ER visit, to OR, sometimes in minutes. Trauma cases are always different. I used to say, "Never criticize a trauma surgery. You weren't there." Here is where you hope you have learned the principles of the musculoskeletal system and a rational approach to orthopaedic problems, both in residency and through experience, that will allow you to apply those principles and do competent surgery.

That said, the "unexpected" comes up more than occasionally. Either the problem is different than what you expected or something happens, you slip, you can't see, a blood vessel bursts, a bone cracks and splinters, hardware gets stuck and you can't get it out. You still have to apply those same principles to fix what you can and have the judgement to quit before more harm than good is done. Here is where the principle of "Good judgement comes from experience. Experience comes from bad judgment" applies.

I always thought you should want somebody five to fifteen years into practice doing your surgery. They have obtained that experience, but they're not too old to be out of date. One way to tell is if the surgeon suddenly says, "Is anybody else hot in here?" and nobody else has noticed a change. You can be sure, that surgeon just had a rush of adrenaline and is worried about something.

That is a terrible feeling. "How am I going to get out of this mess?" Not fun.

I remember one time doing a proximal tibial osteotomy where I thought I had plunged an osteotome into major blood vessels in the leg. The tourniquet was up so there wasn't a gush of blood, but I still was terrified. It turned out I didn't, but those are moments of sheer terror! Don't begrudge your surgeon some extra compensation for dealing with this stress without a chance to go research it. They have to make decisions now. You don't want a wishy washy surgeon.

Can the line be crossed from confident and decisive to egotistical and arrogant? Yup. It happens more than occasionally. That's why those personality traits are attracted to surgery and that's why surgeons can have that reputation. I'm not excusing it and there's the matter of degrees, but that helps explain some of it.

There are some doctors to watch out for. Some are just not good people. For years, doctors have had their bad behavior tolerated, particularly in the OR. Maybe it's because they are "captain of the ship" (which they are), but some take it to an extreme, throwing instruments, yelling and being nasty to the staff. There is no way this should be tolerated. But it still is. Thankfully, it's not near as bad as in past years. "The OR is just so stressful" is not a legitimate reason. It's stressful for all doctors and not all of them act this way.

Some insufferable jerks are very good doctors. It's a conundrum in many ways. Complaining will get you somewhere, but not as far as being nice.

"YOU WHAT?" Moments from Surgery

The first place we get "YOU WHAT?" moments for surgery are in the pre-operative area where the nurses are getting final information and preparing the patient for the surgery itself.

The questions can elicit some interesting answers:

"Have you had anything to eat or drink this morning?" (They are supposed to have nothing after midnight, maybe some clear liquids in the morning.)

1. "No" said the patient, a 20-year-old male. "No, but he smoked crystal meth on the way over here this morning." His mother ratted him out. Good thing. Meth in the system plus general anesthesia can be quite dangerous. Surgery was canceled.

2. "Yes. I drank Gatorade at six, eight and ten and in the waiting room before surgery."

3. "Yes. I woke myself up and ate grapes at 4am because a nurse friend of mine said I could eat grapes."

4. "Yes. I had a burger and fries." "YOU WHAT? Why would you do that?" "Well, they told me I couldn't eat breakfast, but I don't eat hamburgers for breakfast."

5. "Yes. I ate a bagel." "A bagel? Why would you eat a bagel?!" The nurse in the office said I could have clear liquids. How do I know they are clear liquids? Just put it up to the light and see if you can read through it."

One patient forgot he had told both his wife and his girlfriend when and where he was having his surgery. They both showed up at the same time. They each introduced themselves. Oops.

Very awkward!

Before every surgery, the CRNA and/or anesthesiologist comes in to discuss anesthesia with the patient. I once asked the CRNA how they decided how much preoperative sedation they gave for relaxation. There were several answers:

1. "I give Versed 0.5 mg per allergy!"

2. "Versed 1 mg per plastic surgery procedure they've had."

3. "1.5 times the normal amount if they have a lot of tattoos."

Humorous stories

One of my favorite stories of all time in the OR is the older lady, a little overweight, who was struggling to transfer from the stretcher to the OR table. The CRNA said "Just lift your hips up and over, Up and over. Up and over. She said, "Honey, my husband has been dead for ten years. I forgot all those moves." We all just cracked up uncontrollably. When I went out to talk to her family afterwards, I didn't mention it, of course. But her daughter asked, "She didn't say anything embarrassing as she was going to sleep, did she?"

To confirm the correct location for any surgery, we now write "Yes" on the site of the surgery with a Sharpie. One day, I walked in and looked at the knee we were going to operate on and I saw the word "Sex." I asked, "Why did you write sex on your knee?" (Orthopaedic guys don't deal much with that.) He said, "I didn't. I wrote Yes."

Horrible stories-Bears in the Woods

We have a saying: "There are bears in the woods." It means, lurking out there are terrible things that can happen without any warning. You can be moving along, everything normal and then disaster happens.

Sometimes you have an inkling. Patients in poor health, having surgery under dire circumstances, can crash. Sometimes they come back and there's no harm done. Sometimes they come back and there are repercussions. Sometimes they die. Unfortunately, it's part of taking care of sick people. Sometimes things just happen that are nobody's fault. They just happen. And sometimes, it's your fault. Totally.

I did that. I operated on the wrong knee!! It's embarrassing to reveal this. It was a routine Friday afternoon. I'm doing my second case after an uneventful first arthroscopy of the knee and the recovery room nurse puts his head in the room and says, "Dr. Chase, about your first patient." I thought, "Is she having some medical problems? Bleeding?" No. "She says you did the wrong knee!"

My first thought was, it's a joke. One patient tried to do that to me before (not funny), but this patient didn't seem the type. Talk about somebody pulling the rug out from underneath you. This was the whole floor. I suddenly felt sick, nauseated, sweaty, clammy, like I had a sudden onset of the flu.

"Let me finish this case and I will come into recovery and look at it."

Easier said than done. I'm not sure how I did it. Concentrating on the surgery I was presently involved with was nearly impossible. Every fiber of me was looking for something to explain this away. But there was no other explanation. The post-op dressings were on the wrong knee. Shit, shit, shit!

I talked to the patient and the family and explained how, indeed, we operated on the wrong knee. (How hard was that to do?) Her options were to get her over this and do the correct knee sometime in the future. Or, do the correct knee today and get the original problem over and rehab both of them. This would take longer and be more difficult, but at least she could concentrate on getting well. So that's what we did.

Ironically the wrong knee had a worse tear of the meniscus than the correct knee, so that's why nothing raised an alarm during the surgery itself. We admitted her to the hospital to make sure the extra surgery and anesthesia didn't cause medical complications. She eventually recovered, with relief of her symptoms, so no damage.

How does that happen? It seems impossible for the lay public to imagine. All surgeons know it could happen to any one of us. We did root cause analysis to see why it happened. In this case, everything was done correctly up until the operating room door closed. It wasn't just one thing. It was a combination of circumstances. I was distracted by a conversation. Just like distracted driving, disaster can happen. The circulating nurse, whose job it is to look after patient safety, was leaving town the next week and had basically checked out and filled out all the papers prior to the surgery, but really didn't check. The scrub tech said, "That's not my job and I never look." So, multiple people didn't do their job right. It could have been prevented if even one of us was paying proper attention.

We since have implemented a number of additional precautions, including a "timeout" to confirm all aspects of preparation, like airline pilots do. But I am the one who is responsible and I accepted that responsibility. I don't blame anybody else. I am the "captain of the ship" and the responsibility falls on my shoulders. As President Harry Truman said in 1953, "The buck stops here." I screwed up, plain and simple.

It was the lowest moment of my life! Period! I was sick, and inconsolable. I said at the time, and my mind hasn't changed, I would have rather gotten cancer again (I had a radical prostatectomy for prostate cancer ten years earlier) than do this. Getting cancer isn't my fault. Wrong site surgery is my fault.

The hardest part for me was questioning my own competence, which I value more than almost anything else in the world, and thinking my family, my staff and my practice partners would question my competence. Amy Evans, a very kind and caring risk manager with our medical malpractice carrier talked with me several times and talked me off the cliff. She sent me information about "the second victim." Basically, we as health care professionals (most of us) take these things so personally that a mistake of this proportion is devastating. And indeed, it was.

It took me a long time to take it off the forefront and stop obsessing about it. I was quite shaken the first time I went back into the OR after that. It's like driving by the scene of a car accident you caused where somebody was badly hurt.

I spent a lot of time with this lady trying to help her recover from this and she stuck with me. But the inevitable happened and we started getting letters from lawyers. That was money too easy to pass up. It's called a *Res Ipsa Loquitur*. The thing speaks for itself. We settled before a lawsuit was actually filed. There were also sanctions from the state. No way around it. When you do something like that, you just take your medicine. There is nothing to fight. It was quite devastating and humbling for me. It was the worst single moment of my life!

Obesity

One of the biggest problems we face as orthopaedic surgeons is obesity. Certainly, for the patients. Much of the poor health in our country can be attributed to or is exacerbated by obesity. But it's also a problem for us in the OR. It's sometimes just physically hard to get them on or off the table when they are asleep. You just need muscle, and lots of it. Particularly if they have to be put in the prone position (on their stomach). Sometimes you don't have enough people and you just lift anyway, causing physical injury to yourself or particularly the staff.

Then, doing the surgery is difficult, challenging and demanding. Sometimes you can't find landmarks to know where to make the incision. It's not just the weight. It's the amount of weight that is jammed into that package, especially if they are short. Once the incision is made you can't see. It is a really deep hole. Sometimes you can't reach that far with your hand or fingers. And sometimes you just can't do it, or you don't do it as well. The fat physically precludes you from doing what you need to do. There are now hard stops on certain weights of patients to do total joint replacements. Not to mention the medical complications that are much more common as obesity increases.

When you see an obese patient, you automatically know how difficult everything is going to be. But it's not like diving or gymnastics. There are no increased points (or reimbursement) given when the degree of difficulty is so high.

I tended to have a reputation for having lots of obese people. Maybe because I wouldn't blow them off immediately when I saw them and they tended to drift toward me or not leave me. One time, one of the scrubs asked me, "Dr. Chase, do you leave your business card at the Golden Corral Buffet?"

You Won't Believe This

Another patient was being quite nasty to all the people preparing her for her surgery. It got to the point where I had to speak to her about it. I said "You can't talk to these people that way. They are just doing their job." Her response "These people here are just the leftovers. If they were any good they would be at the hospital." My response "Well then, you are not having surgery here if you are going to act like this. And I am not doing surgery on you anywhere!" What she didn't realize is that the people there at the surgery center were the best, or they wouldn't make it there. They were certainly more experienced. New grads always start at the hospital where they get trained, just like residents.

Late in my career, we counted up the years of experience the people in the operating room had. The four people in the room - surgeon, nurse, CRNA and scrub tech - had over 120 years of experience. It was quite reassuring to have them in there with me.

One time, I met the patient's wife in the pre-op area, but couldn't find her after the surgery. After the surgery, I asked the nurses where she was. They said, "She is in the parking lot. She doesn't want to talk to you about him." Why? "He wouldn't give his cell phone to his wife while he was under anesthesia."

People Die

People can die in or after surgery. The anesthesia and the surgery itself is a stress to the system. We do everything we can to minimize the risk, but if you are around long enough, you hear stories of people dying totally unexpectedly during or after surgery. And they can increase those chances if they don't give us good information or the right information. Like not mentioning you smoked crystal meth on the way to surgery. Or, that your two siblings have major bleeding problems in surgery. Or, you need blood transfusions on a regular basis. When I asked, "FOR WHAT?" they replied, "Oh, I forgot to write down my leukemia."

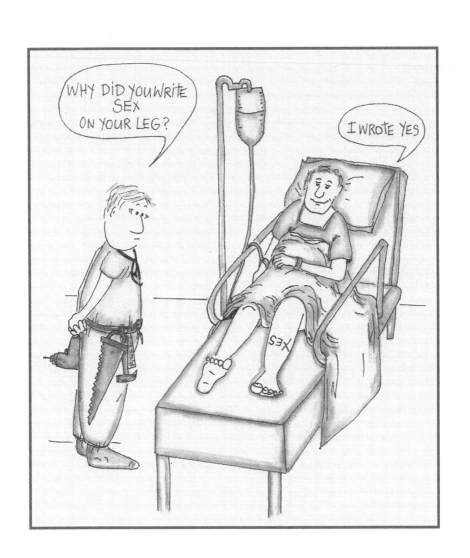

CHAPTER 7
CHARACTERISTICS OF A
GOOD DOCTOR

Let's go into the doctor's lounge and meet some of the good doctors. How can you tell? You can't tell by looking. Some of the best are rather unimposing. Dumpy, not well dressed, maybe with not a lot of social skills. They are probably not glad handing, shaking other doctor's hands, self-promoting, working the crowd to get more referrals.

I've learned over the years that there are good people and bad people, good doctors and bad doctors and they are not necessarily synonymous. It is not a 100% correlation. What you want is good people who are good doctors and there are lots of them. The same characteristics that make good people correlate pretty well with being a good doctor. There are good people who are not good doctors, but not many.

In this chapter I am using a female as an example of the good doctor because, in my experience, on the whole, women are the better of the two genders.

Knows Her Stuff

The first and most important thing is the doctor has to "know her stuff." She has to have a knowledge base and the ability to think and reason. She has to have good judgement in applying that knowledge. It used to be you had to have all that in your head, but now much can be looked up and rather quickly. But you still have to recognize warning signs and put the pieces together.

You want a smart doctor who went to a good medical school and residency, who keeps up and has good judgement. That's all! Easy! That is "necessary, but not sufficient" to be a good doctor.

Nice Guy

People frequently say, "I don't care what his personality is like, I just want somebody good." Particularly with surgeons. You want somebody that knows how and is technically proficient enough to do your operation well. But you would be surprised. Listen to when people talk about their doctors. "She's a really nice doctor." Doctors do the same thing. "Who would you recommend going to for such and such a problem?" "Go to Tom Smith. He's a really nice guy." And they should know. And, they still use this criteria.

Not often, but occasionally you might hear "Go to Tom Smith. He's a jerk, but he's a good surgeon." So, if you are really, really good, you might get away with being a jerk, but being nice to people does matter, even for doctors.

What Makes a Good Doctor?

When I had medical students with me, I used to tell them, "You don't have to be brilliant to be a good doctor. If you got here, you are plenty smart. You didn't do well with all that schooling and those hard courses by being a dummy. You just need to be conscientious and responsible. Do the right thing every time. Dot all I's and cross all T's. Check all the boxes. Check on the little things that might make the difference."

We have an old saying, "When you hear hoof beats, think horses, not zebras." You might not pick up the ultra-rare disease. But that's what the smart guys at the Mayo Clinic are for. You just need to do a good job with the regular stuff.

Good Doctors Do These Things

All good doctors don't have all these things, but the more you have, the better. I realize these things are opinions, but it's my book. My opinions. So, let's follow that good doctor through the day and see what she does. It's probably no coincidence that we are following a female as they are usually better people than the males and have more of these characteristics. Sad but true. Testosterone is an evil substance.

She woke up after a good night's sleep. She did all the right things yesterday so she wasn't worried that she missed things and they didn't roil around in her head all night and keep her up.

She makes rounds at the hospital and listens to the nurses. They spent the night with the patient and a good nurse can pick up when a patient is (or is about to be) in trouble long before any numbers in the stupid EMR picks it up.

She is nice to the nurses (and the techs and the cleaning people). She treats them with respect. She says please and thank you.

She leaves plenty of time for the unexpected, which is expected. You just don't know in what form. She is not late to the office. That is something you can never catch up from. She balances the productivity vs enough time with the patient conundrum.

She leaves enough time to review the schedule and the tests she ordered that she will be reviewing with each of her patients. She can do some research if she needs to. She may have even done this the day or two before. In a word, she is prepared!

Her schedule is reasonable. There are always unexpected calls from the hospital, patients, and administrators and she leaves time for them. She doesn't take all the calls that come in, just the necessary ones and messages are taken.

There are always patients with something you have allotted ten minutes for and they need 20 minutes. She has factored that in. She is respectful of her patient's time and tries to stay on schedule. (This is the real art: giving the patients the time they need and making them feel it was enough. Those are sometimes two very different things.)

She sees her new patients. She walks into the room. She smiles. It makes a huge difference.

She listens, really listens, to the patient. (Remember that 40 second thing?) She looks them in the eye. Never trust a doctor who won't look you in the eye. (The new electronic medical records and typing and box clicking make this very difficult, if she has been turned into a transcriptionist as well as a doctor.) She uses humor if possible and when appropriate. She reads people and their nonverbal clues well.

She examines her patient. She touches them. You would not believe the number of Doctors who don't touch the patient on their visit. Their excuse is, "It doesn't matter. I make my decisions on the studies." Maybe. But the patient still wants to feel like they mattered and an exam involves touching them.

She then discusses diagnosis and treatment. She figures out what the patient is there for and addresses that. She is concise and effective when she speaks. She has learned to artfully give bad news. She is conservative. She doesn't jump into new things just because they are new. As I mentioned before, new and approved is not necessarily new and improved.

There is always the law of unintended consequences. Unless it is really an emergency, she arranges to have them come back for follow up to get a better idea of what that patient is really like. Is this someone she should operate on or not.? And, not now or not ever? She recognizes crazy (hopefully) and steers clear.

She then sees her follow up patients. Anybody can see the patients that are doing well. They are easy. They are happy and it doesn't take very long. She feels pretty good leaving that room. The ones that aren't doing well, they are hard. Maybe temporarily. Maybe permanently. The key thing is, she cares. These struggling patients need more time, not less. She takes the time they need so they don't feel abandoned, even if she can't do anything. She knows what is important and keeps the patient focused on that rather than isolated irritations that occur in any post-op course. She learns not to take everything so personally, especially how the patient does.

She makes good decisions. Some of those follow up patients are there to discuss surgery. A surgeon is like a quarterback or a point guard. Their success is determined by the decisions they make. Who to operate on and who to not operate on. This can be very tough. Whether she has made a good decision or not may not be evident for weeks or months. A poor decision can be misery for months or years, for her as well as the patient.

She is humble, not arrogant. She tries not to take too much credit for when things go well so she doesn't have to take the blame when they don't. She sets realistic expectations. It may be the most important thing she does. There are problems that just can't be made whole. The results you were hoping for may just be better, but not normal. If that is the case and you don't let the patient know that in advance, you may get a very unhappy patient. You want to give them confidence, without unrealistic expectations.

She never minds a second opinion. No good surgeon minds. If the patient thinks that you are talking them into something and it doesn't go perfectly, you are the bad guy. If they want to go somewhere else, let them. If they didn't have the confidence to go ahead with you before, they certainly are not going to get it later. The problem is when they get a second opinion or third opinion and they are all different. Then you just tell them, "Go with what makes the most sense to you and the person you have the most confidence in and don't second guess yourself."

Next, she is off for surgery. Wait, maybe not. The patient listed as follow up knee arthritis is really there for a large lump in their thigh, probably cancer. That is not a short discussion. And, scheduling put three new patients in follow up slots. New patients always take way longer than follow ups. A post-op patient called in with problems. She worked them in that morning. You have to. If they have problems and you don't see them, you are cooked when the depositions start.

The last patient would not stop talking! The office manager needs to speak with you about something and she appropriately didn't interrupt her with this while seeing patients. She is now running behind because no matter how much you have prepared, something always happens.

The operating room where she is going knows this. Surgeons being late for surgery is quite common. But this good doctor calls and lets them know she will be late and a realistic time for being there. It is just polite and it gives them the flexibility to move things around in surgery.

In the OR

Now, she has made it to the OR and there are a few blips. The doctor in the room ahead of her is running over again for the third week in a row! But she doesn't decompensate and yell at the OR staff. It's not their fault. When they are ready in the room, she is immediately ready and does not waste everybody's time by having conversations in the hall or lingering on business phone conversations.

She goes into the room, greets everybody by name (she has worked with them for years) and helps move the patient on and off the table and helps with the draping. Sometimes, things don't go well in the OR. It is a struggle for multiple reasons. The patient is very heavy and she is having the proverbial technical difficulty. We use lots of equipment, some very sophisticated and computer driven and occasionally, there are glitches.

And sometimes, something goes wrong. Something is cut that wasn't supposed to be cut, something is broken or just can't be fixed. She is calm and collected and assess her options, redirects and finds another way to get the job done.

If the case is not going well for some reason she does not take it out on the staff by yelling at them. She knows they are trying their best and yelling at them only puts everybody in the room on edge. She knows that everyone in the room is truly trying to help make things go as smoothly as possible. (Why wouldn't they? They get to go home sooner as well.) When the case is over she helps get the dressings on and of course helps get the unconscious patient (who might be very heavy, there are a lot of them these days) off the table and on to the stretcher.

There. See how easy that is?

"YOU WHAT?" Moments from Good Doctors

Doctors need good doctors too! I was getting a physical in 2003 and in reviewing the lab work, John Ryan, my internist said, "Your PSA is a little high. I would suggest seeing a urologist about it." I looked at the lab sheet with him and said, "I don't see any stars here. It all looks normal to me. What do I need to see a urologist for?"

He was very patient with this *know it all* orthopaedic surgeon and said, "Technically, that is correct, but your PSA is too high for your age and you might want to have it looked at." So, I saw the urologist, just to pacify my internist and we did a biopsy and sure enough, I had Prostate Cancer, Gleason grade 6 in 10/12 cores of the biopsy. We talked about options, of which there were many.

I had always said, "If I got cancer (or anything bad), I would go with a 'full court press' (good basketball analogy) and be very aggressive about trying to get a cure. If that didn't work, then maybe I'd make other decisions and not keep beating a dead horse.

I decided to have it surgically removed, but wasn't too keen on sitting in stirrups with my perineum in the air in the hospital in which I practiced and knew everybody. My urologist, Dave Vaughn, suggested if I wanted to go out of town to some guru at some big center for prostate cancer, he would be willing to take care of all the post op care and follow up so I wouldn't have to fly to Chicago for every little thing.

I know what a generous offer that was. It is a pet peeve for surgeons when patients decide to go elsewhere for a surgery you are perfectly qualified to do. Then they show up in your office for routine care, that doctor is too far to drive or for complications.

It makes us mad. If I'm not good enough to take care of your original problem, then why am I suddenly good enough to take care of the complications of a surgery that I might not have done in the first place?

For Dave to offer to do that was very magnanimous and greatly appreciated. Seventeen years later, I am still cancer free and don't even think about it. I am still alive and I sure have slept better because of these two good doctors in their knowledge and willingness to help me out.

Grateful Patient

You never know who or what will show up in the office and where it might take you. Twenty-five years ago, Rita showed up in the office with her 20-year-old daughter Karie who had been in a car accident two weeks before. She had an injury to her ankle, but no fractures and the doctors in the trauma center sutured her laceration. The sutures were out now, but something didn't seem right to them. After examination, I said, "I think you had some lacerations to some of the tendons in the front of the ankle and your ankle is never going to move normally if they aren't repaired. But we are two weeks out now and I don't know how well they will come together or how well they will heal. I recommend we at least give it a try."

Does that inspire a lot of confidence in you? Would you let some doctor you had never met before take your daughter for semi-urgent surgery for a problem that he said may not go very well? (Be honest, but you don't want to hear that pessimistic crap when it is your child.) We did take her to surgery and the tendons were able to be put back together and they healed. I didn't know that going in. They sometimes can retract and you can't get them together. She was able to get back to full normal activity, thank God! Only repercussions were a very large scar on the front of her ankle.

The Rackleys came back to see me for years for everything orthopaedic. Rita brought her husband to me for his knee, son in law and herself for their knees. It was one of those great long-term relationships with a family that primary care people have a lot of, but not usually orthopaedic surgeons.

It turned out, Jon and Rita owned a nursery. I asked our landscaper when we were redoing all the plants in our yard one time if he knew them and he said of course. They were one of the best nurseries around and he would use them for the plants. When it came time to pay the landscaper, he gave us the bill and it seemed way too small. I said, "This should be much more than this." He said, "You are right, but Rita said you weren't paying for any plants from their farm!"

Two weeks before I retired, Karie came in for something else orthopaedic. At the end of the visit, I told her I was retiring and she started crying. She said, "Who are my family and I going to go to when you are gone?" I started crying too! I'm tearing up right now.

Mentor to me

I went to the University of Florida for my residency in 1980 and I didn't know a soul in Gainesville. But I chose that residency for their emphasis on teaching and not being "a knife and gun club," a term used for so much trauma that you didn't do anything else but operate. I was right. It was a great choice. We had a daily conference schedule where we as residents presented cases, heard lectures and were grilled with questions designed to make us think and reason, not to belittle us or to make us look stupid. This is called the Socratic teaching method and it was (and is) very effective.

If you are actively engaged in learning, you remember much more than if you are being lectured to. It has long been proven that your memory is much better when those memories are attached to emotion (even anxiety, terror, and embarrassment).

There was one particular faculty member named Dempsey Springfield who was very laid back, but when he spoke or asked a question, we were on high alert because we knew we had to think. And he would pop in little gems, old stories, and aphorisms, to make his point. Many of the philosophies I pass along in this book came directly from him, particularly about a conservative approach to surgery.

What I learned from him was that your contribution to the orthopaedic health of your community, state or world is so much greater if you teach. There are large numbers and multiple generations of students who can learn from you and use that knowledge to better the health of their communities. There's more value to your career than just pounding out surgeries one at a time. That's good, but it's limited.

One of my fellow residents said, "You know, when we are out in practice and deciding what we are going to do for a patient, there will be a little Dempsey Springfield on our shoulders whispering into our ears, "Are you sure you want to do that?" I can think of no finer tribute.

Mentor to Others

One of the things I am most proud of in my career was winning the Hugh Hill award at the University of Florida Medical School when I was a fourth-year resident. The plaque says, "The house officer best exemplifying the leader, teacher, clinician and friend for whom this award was named. Presented by the Class of 1984."

So in 2005, when Florida State University Medical School enrolled its first class, I knew I wanted to be involved. I was one of the several orthopaedic surgeons in Orlando who became clinical faculty for junior, and later senior, medical students as they did their clinical rotations in Orlando. I would have them for usually two to four weeks and might share them with another orthopaedist.

It was different as clinical faculty than when I was a resident. I now had responsibility. I was getting paid and I had to fill out evaluations on the students. To do it right, you have to spend some time and effort. The student can't be expected to just observe you and be in awe of your clinical and surgical skills. Especially junior students need to learn the transition between being a regular person and being a professional. You have to think differently. So, I tried to use that same Socratic teaching method with my students. I put them on the spot when they were presenting patients. I worked with them (sometimes very painfully) to get them to make clear and concise presentations. I made them look up topics and present them to me. I made them look up information on patients that we saw in the clinic. I helped them learn about orthopaedic emergencies and the common things their families will call them about.

Some of them didn't appreciate it. One of my evaluations said, "Dr. Chase didn't have any understanding about us having a test at the end of this rotation." Some of them loved it, especially the ones who wanted to do orthopaedics. I met some great people I would be very happy to have taking care of me as my orthopaedic surgeon. But my favorite student was an unassuming female who was thinking about obstetrician-gynecologist (OB/GYN). Her name was Princess Urbina. I thought, "This girl will never be a surgeon. With a name like Princess they will tear her up."

But she was very interested, despite knowing she wouldn't go into orthopaedics. I gave her topics to research and she came back with a presentation with notes and a summary of the important facts about this subject (which were so good I kept and used for my other students). She worked hard at her presentations and couldn't get enough. She actively sought feedback on "How can I improve?" and wanted me to be tough on her. "That's how I will learn." I loved this girl. We began to talk throughout the rotation about career goals and I encouraged her to go for it, because, despite my initial impression, I thought she could be a great surgeon!

I gave her this feedback and then, like all students do, she went away. And the next week, others come in for their rotations. The difference with her was that a year later, I received this text. I almost never heard back from previous students, except occasionally from ones that went into orthopaedics. Here's what she sent me:

"Good evening Dr. Chase. I wanted to say thank you for being so encouraging during my rotation with you. I decide to pursue a career in OBGyn and am thrilled to share that I matched into my #1 choice at the George Washington University in DC. I couldn't have done this without your encouragement and support. Endless thanks."

I can't tell you how much that meant to me! As we never delete anything from our phones anymore, two years later I texted her to let her know I had retired and was writing a book and a blog. Her reply warmed my heart again. She said, "I've decided to apply to minimally invasive Gyn Surgery fellowships. Please know you have significantly impacted my career and I will always remember you encouraging me to be 'twice as good' as those around me."

This is for you, Dempsey Springfield. Your heritage continues to be passed down.

Humorous Story

I was sometimes a pain in the ass for my office staff. I was "pathologically punctual." I was never late and usually came in early, really early. I would check future weeks to see what surgeries had been added and look at the schedule in the office for the day to see who was coming in. Sometimes I would know the patients on the list, sometimes not.

There are people who you never forget and when you see their name on the schedule you go "Oh crap" and you know your morning is ruined.

One morning, I began to look at the list and when I saw the first patient I said, "Ugh." Second patient, I said, "Oh no." Third patient, out came "Crap!" And it kept going. I was getting depressed and the farther along the list I got, the angrier I got. "They should know not to put all these complicated people in the same morning. Each one of them is going to take forever. I am never going to make it to surgery on time!" (Did I mention I am pathologically punctual?) But then I saw the last patient listed, the worst combination of difficult problem, difficult patient and endless questions that she would repeat over and over again, followed by crying and her husband rubbing her shoulders. I burst out "Not Deborah Jorgensen!!!" (Not her real name.)

About then, my nurse and scheduler came in and I went apoplectic, ranting and raving about what a terrible schedule this was and who did this and what were they thinking? They stood there very quietly, taking it all in until I finished. Then in unison they said, "April Fools! Dr. Chase."

They got me! And I deserved it. Good one! Meredith Wiggins, our office manager, declined all participation because, in her words, "I don't want to have any part of his heart attack."

CHAPTER 8
CHARACTERISTICS OF BAD DOCTORS
- DON'T BE LIKE THIS!

Now, let's go across the hall to where a bad doctor practices. And they can be that close. There are, of course, degrees. Not all "not great doctors" are bad. As I mentioned, you want a smart doctor who went to a good medical school and residency, who keeps up and has good judgement. That is necessary, but not sufficient to be a good doctor. A bad doctor can fail in a number of those categories.

It is very hard for a doctor to be dumb as they usually don't make it through the process to get there. Lots of good, smart people don't make it into medical school because the competition is so tough. Keeping up requires effort. You have to read about your patients and the appropriate journals in your field. A bad doctor is lazy and won't do the work to keep up their knowledge base and keep up with new information. Old saying: "You don't know what you don't know." As far as good judgement goes, that is really hard to measure.

First of all, we have to distinguish between bad people and bad doctors.

Bad Doctors

You can have good people who, for some reason, lose their way. They are overworked (perhaps their own doing, perhaps forced upon them by administrators.) They may be depressed, burnt out, have family problems, their wife is leaving them, their kids have to be put in rehab, all through seemingly no fault of their own. Nobody ever really knows.

Or it may be entirely their fault. They may have financial woes. One of my maxims for living has been, "Never make financial commitments that require ever escalating income." Or they may be having an extramarital affair. Doctors are prime targets for gold-diggers.

The bottom line is they are not directing their full attention to their practice and their patients suffer for it. They are not bad people. As my friend Mike MacMillan once said, "They are running downhill and it's getting steeper every step."

Sometimes they just get lazy. They forget or just don't bother to check on that culture or lab result. They don't check the chart before they walk into the room and have that patient confused with somebody else. You can't remember everything about everybody. That's why we have charts. Take a minute to check it before you walk in. You will give better patient care and you won't look like an uncaring idiot to your patient.

Recognize Limitations

For surgeons, you have to be able to recognize your limitations. Not everybody is Jimmy Andrews, a world-renowned guru who people fly to see from all over the country when they "want the best." (When somebody says to me "I want the best," I tell them "Well, let me refer to someone else.") First, my ego doesn't require that stroking and that kind of patient is never going to be satisfied.

We all have an ego that makes us look at a surgery and say, "I can do that." Maybe. Maybe not. Testosterone is an evil substance and convinces lots of us that we can do things that we really can't. This happens in both sports and surgery. Some of my most grateful patients have written me very nice letters after treatment elsewhere, thanking me for getting them to where it would be best for them.

A bad doctor doesn't take into account other factors besides those that are on the data (x-rays , MRI's, labs) when deciding whether to offer that patient surgery for this problem. A frankly crazy patient may not do well, despite you doing the most technically beautiful surgery ever. You have to recognize that.

Realistic Expectations

So, you decide you can do the surgery, but it's tricky and a little risky. You have to give the patient realistic ideas of what can and can't be accomplished. There are some problems that can be fixed and they get 100% better. These patients are very happy, never come back and tell all their friends what a wonderful surgeon you are. That's the best. However, there are lots of problems where there is so much damage before you do the surgery that the only reasonable goal is to mitigate the damage and improve things as much as possible. But the patient doesn't know the difference between those problems and you do. It's your job to help them understand that difference so they can have realistic expectations. If you don't do that before the surgery, you are setting yourself up for a disappointed patient and a miserable doctor who says, "Oh no!" every time they see them on the schedule.

And then there's the surgeon with an overinflated ego or is lazy who doesn't prepare properly and "wings it," like the commercial that says, "We'll figure it out when we are in there." There are indeed, times when you have to do that. But it shouldn't be because you haven't prepared. The bottom line is that these doctors are not conscientious and responsible.

Bad People

Then there are the doctors who are not good people and can run the gamut of being good doctors to terrible ones.

Unindicated Operations on Unsuspecting People

First, the easy ones. These people do unindicated operations on unsuspecting people just to make money. I hold my biggest contempt for these people. Fortunately, there aren't many of them. They get picked up pretty quick by the medical community and/or intelligent patients or medical boards because their actions are so egregious.

If you operate on a self-limited problem and it goes away after your surgery (which it would have anyway), you can look pretty good, as long as you don't have a lot of complications. The really bad ones consider lawsuits a risk of doing business and factor it in. No big deal. They have expensive lawyers who fight in court and in the Board of Medicine disciplinary proceedings and threaten lawsuits and wheel and deal and can stay in practice a long time. I can thankfully say, there are not a lot of these around.

Aggressive Indications

The harder ones to figure out are the surgeons with "aggressive indications." Medicine, surgery and orthopaedic surgery all have a lot of latitude for different opinions. There is usually more than one way to approach a patient's problem. My philosophy is to learn what constitutes emergencies and with everything else, treat them in a stepwise fashion with increasing levels of surgical indications if the problem gets worse or what you are doing is not working. Pretty simplistic, but not a bad approach.

But, there are some surgeons who recommend surgery and the most aggressive (lucrative?) kind right off the bat. A "good salesman" can make anything sound good. When the indications are reviewed, the reviewer says, "Well, yeah, you can make an argument for that, but it's a little aggressive." And there you are. Full operative schedule and a "successful" practice.

They are not bad doctors. Indications are within established guidelines, if a little aggressive, but you are not going to get a real chance at conservative management. And some people don't want that. They want what is going to solve the problem right away. All well and good, unless there are complications

A lot of doctors are hung up on money. A lot of people are hung up on money. Doctors are people (usually). Shouldn't be too surprising. But I was surprised. I thought, quite naively, that most doctors didn't care a lot about money. They just wanted to do a good job for their patients and be comfortable. Now, don't get me wrong. I think physicians should be compensated well for what they do. They are bright people, hard workers and if they took those skills anywhere else they would be compensated handsomely.

I don't think most doctors start out so preoccupied with money. I don't remember my medical school classmates talking about the big money they were going to make when they got out. Doctors are very good at delayed gratification. They spend most of their time studying in college and medical school. They get paid a pittance in residency and work 80 or more hours a week. There is always their reward, finally, waiting out there when they finish. Think about it. Their college classmates in marketing partied hearty in college, got crap for grades, and got a good job in sales and were making good money 11-12 years before these doctors were finally able to earn a good paycheck. That is pent up consumerism. No wonder they think about money.

The other thing I think that happens is now they are suddenly in a peer group who has money and is talking about what they are doing with it. You begin to think, maybe I should be doing this. The problem is in the comparison! A "successful practice" is just another name for a lucrative one. And that's when they start thinking about more and more ways to get more money.

After a few years in practice, I would start thinking, "Maybe I should be doing some of these things" and start getting jealous. Then I would ask myself "What would my friends from high school and college say if they heard me complaining about what I am getting paid?" I think money is like a drug you get habituated to. You need more and more to satisfy that ever growing need. A favorite quote of mine is, "No doctor has an income problem. If there is not enough money, they have a spending problem."

And, I think money changes you. Not everybody, but some. "I deserve it," they say and stop at nothing to get it. They get unethical in outside business dealings and start doing things they never would have imagined getting out of residency.

Good doctors but...

There are plenty of really good physicians that you would want to be in charge of your medical care, but would not want to be friends with or have your daughter go out with them. Some are just inconsiderate. They don't respect their patient's time. And they do that to other doctors too. They over schedule, but don't care if they make the doctor behind them late.

Reasonable doctors, if they know they have made somebody late, will come out, apologize and explain why they got behind. The inconsiderate ones just sneak out the back door.

There are varying degrees of dishonesty. This can go from using "stat" every time they order things. Rarely is there "stat" in orthopaedics. Your add-on surgical cases are always an emergency. "I have to do it this afternoon!" (Because they have concert tickets that night.) If you do this frequently enough, you lose your credibility and nobody believes you when you say something is an emergency. There is nothing more important than your credibility. Dishonesty can evolve into lying to patients and staff and the unforgivable sin: changing medical records. You get caught doing this, you can just settle and sign the check in your malpractice trial.

Arrogance

Some doctors are arrogant. They don't believe anybody else can be right and their opinion is always correct. They are dismissive of any other opinion. They are critical of other physician's work, which is a bad idea because "You weren't there, particularly in surgery." One time I was trying to fix an open fracture of a tibia at 2AM and it was a mess. I couldn't get it back together the way I wanted it no matter how hard I tried. I knew the X-ray was going to look terrible and I said to myself, "I will never criticize somebody else's fracture work because I was not there." Until you know all the facts, you should shut your mouth until you get all the information.

Mean

Some doctors are just mean and they treat people terribly. One particular doctor I remember cracked inappropriate and tasteless comments to staff and other physicians alike. He thought, "They just have to put up with it because I'm the surgeon." It eventually led to his dismissal.

This is a great example of one of my favorite sayings, "The character of a person can best be gleaned from how they treat people they don't think can do anything for them."

Sexual Harassment

Some are sexual harassers. It never has been okay, but these days women don't have to put up with it like they maybe did before. Some take it farther and become unfaithful to their spouse. How many lies did they have to tell to pull off that affair? When you get good at lying, maybe it leaks over to other facets of your life. It's usually men. Testosterone is an evil substance.

Greedy

Some doctors find ways to profit from the non-patient care side. Outright payments are clearly off base, but there are lots of gray areas. Sometimes it's getting paid to use that prosthesis under the guise of "consulting fees." Some consulting fees are definitely legitimate. The doctor provides legitimate design ideas, but those fees can be way out of proportion to what they really do. If you accept golf or ski weekends, (now outlawed) you can't help but feel some obligation to look favorably on that sales rep and his product. Dates and affairs with sales reps are also not unheard of.

"YOU WHAT?" Moments from Bad Doctors

Bad Patient Experience

This one was very personal. My mom was a very healthy 78-year-old active lady. She'd had one to two weeks of a headache and vague neurological symptoms. A CAT scan showed a subdural hematoma and she was admitted to the hospital for the standard drainage of the hematoma. She was assigned Dr. Jones as her neurosurgeon, as he was on call for emergencies that day. I got there in the afternoon after the surgery and met with the neurosurgeon who said "Everything went great. But we will have to watch her for a stroke."

Everything had not gone great! She had a dense neurological deficit in the recovery room and an emergency CT scan had been ordered which, we later learned, showed blood and air in the brain substance. We were not told about it. A very long story short, she continued to deteriorate, was ignored by her neurosurgeon, who blamed her condition on a stroke. Further studies were done only when ordered by her hospitalist. Dr. Jones ordered a DNR on her without discussing it with any of my family! By this time, she had deteriorated beyond hope and died two weeks later. Dr. Jones had no intention of discussing this with our family until he was forced to by the hospital risk management department. When he did, he blamed it on an assistant for "Forcefully irrigating the brain," which never happened. He even blamed it on somebody who wasn't even in the room at the time of the surgery.

The egregious care she received was beyond anything I had seen or heard of before. An operative event occurred. It can happen. All surgeon's hands can plunge on slippery bloody surfaces. The difference here was 1. He lied about it to the family. 2. He didn't tell any other people on the medical team about what happened so something could be done to mitigate the damage and he did nothing himself. And 3. He ignored her in the hospital, hoping she would die quickly. 4. When caught, he blamed the event on a surgical tech who was nowhere close to the room and would not have done what he was accused of by Dr. Jones.

Our family pursued this aggressively and he lost his hospital privileges and eventually his medical license. Much to our chagrin, it turned out he had multiple episodes of medical negligence and our case was the final blow to his medical career. But to us, he should have never been in the hospital in the first place where he could be assigned to our mother, let alone anyone else. Hard to get much worse than that. And I'm a doctor.

Impacting Team Members

This litany of meanness and arrogance was not one surgeon, but many different surgeons' behavior rolled into one day. But all of these events actually happened:

The surgeon walks into the OR area and announces, "I have a plane to catch at 5PM so we need to hurry up."

The surgeon says to a nurse, "You are too short. You are going to contaminate the field."

"Why do we never have this equipment ready?"

"This piece of crap should never be re-used so I will make it so." He then overreacts and throws the instruments or breaks them.

When the scrub tech was sick and was going to faint, the surgeon says "Fall the other way and don't contaminate the field."

The surgeon says to the scrub tech, "Did your parents raise any intelligent children?"

Another One

A local physician was doing surgery which was quite difficult and taking longer than the two-hour maximum the tourniquet should be on. (We use a tourniquet to obstruct the blood flow to the arm or leg for up to two hours to safely allow a bloodless field and better visualization. That's generally a good idea. Seeing is good in surgery.)

His assistant for the day, another surgeon, told him he read an article that it was okay to leave the tourniquet on for up to four hours and no harm would come to the patient. Definitely not conventional wisdom. So, he left the tourniquet on for three and a hald hours, with the expected poor results. You don't go against conventional wisdom on the hint of some article that somebody might have read that you hear about in the middle of a difficult surgery.

CHAPTER 9

"YOU WHAT?" MOMENTS TO AVOID

There are intricacies to every profession that people who aren't doing that job don't get. "You just don't understand" is a very valid statement. That is what a lot of this book is about. Maybe this will help you have a better understanding of what we do, what we think, and what we fear. I'll start with…

Being On Call

One of the unique things about being in medicine is that you get to be on call. For those of you that don't understand what this means, you work all day, anywhere from 8-12 hours doing surgery, office and paperwork. Then you finish. (Maybe you get to finish. Sometimes it starts before you get done with your regular work.) At 5 o'clock, the phone (used to be beeper) starts ringing.

My friend Mike Macmillan had the best analogy for what it's like to be on call. "Being on call is like standing alone in a dark room, just waiting for something to hit you. You don't know when or from where it will come, you just know that it is coming. Even if you don't get hit, you still have to stand there in the dark for 24 hours and wait. Then at 7 am, somebody comes in and turns on the light again and it is all better. You can finally breathe again."

Sexual Harassment

We, as males, can't make any comments about the appearance of any female. Certainly about any patient, but about our staff, as well. In the #metoo movement era, you can never say, "You look nice today." You never know how it will be received; as a simple complimentary comment or a leering proposal.

This should strike fear into the hearts of all men, and those women who know them and love them. Years, even decades later, someone can make an accusation and it is automatically believed, whether there is any evidence or not, and your life can be ruined! So, we as men, cannot put ourselves in a position to be accused. Be aware of everything you do and say to give yourself the smallest chance of those accusations being leveled at you.

The reason I bring this up is the office environment. We go into a closed room, by ourselves, with females (could be males too, I guess) with varying degrees of clothes on and it would be very, very easy for a disgruntled patient to level an accusation of improper behavior and we are helpless to defend ourselves. Do we now need a chaperone 100% of the time to protect ourselves against those accusations? Maybe.

Having to See Our Predators

Why do we have to see and treat our predators (personal injury lawyers)? In what world can those sharks advertise about our incompetence, implant ideas of our terrible care in the public's heads, threaten us, sue us for frivolous reasons, use the legal system for a shakedown and then turn around and expect us to treat them as if none of that matters because "It's just business?" I'd rather not. That's just how I feel.

Unexpected Things Happen

One time I did a total knee replacement on a lady and came in the next day to find she had signs of a stroke. Our worst fears: a permanent complication related to (or caused by?) our surgery. Her workup showed a brain tumor that was not noticeable before surgery but the surgery stress made it become evident. Knowing that, we would never have done an elective surgery like a total knee. But sometimes, there are surprises.

Denials by Insurance Companies, Medicare and Workman's Comp

One of the things that drove me crazy and was a big factor in me wanting to get out of medicine was denials for what we thought were good indications for medical goods or services. Third parties (Workmen's Compensation, Insurance companies, Medicare) regularly denied goods and services in the effort to save money, instead of doing what was best for the patient.

Government

The government is one of the biggest frustrations to practicing medicine. At best, they think they are trying to help people. At worst, they are busybody bureaucrats who think they know best and stick their noses in the practice of medicine without knowing anything about it.

Classic example: When Hilary Clinton was put in charge of revamping American medicine by her husband, she had zero physicians on her committee. They create regulations, ostensibly to improve things, but then, the law of unintended consequences kicks in and the system they create is worse than when they started.

The Health Insurance Portability Act (HIPAA) is a prime example. Originally intended to improve patient privacy (who could argue with that?), it became a monumental obstruction to efficiency and the ability to take care of patients. We now spend hours of unproductive time meeting those regulations.

Bureaucracy

The levels of bureaucracy we deal with! It's probably not as bad as somebody who works in government. Wait a minute. We do! Just not as overtly.

I gave a patient a prescription for physical therapy after an arthroscopy and a request to return to the clinic in three weeks. They did come back three weeks later. Not because it was time, but because the therapists needed a new prescription. The therapists couldn't get them in for an appointment for three weeks and when the patient came in they said, "The prescription is out of date. You will have to go back to the doctor and get a new prescription." And we want the government to have even more control of our healthcare system where this kind of thing would occur daily?

Legal

This is a huge subject. Hanging over doctors' heads, every day, with every patient, is the threat of getting sued for medical negligence, otherwise known as malpractice. It never leaves our minds. We document, sometimes excessively, because we are told your medical record is your best friend if you get sued. We make decisions all the time that are altered because we are afraid of a lawsuit.

I am the first person to say doctors should be accountable for what they do (see the section on my mother). I am quite upset when I see poor medical care. But there is a difference between an honest mistake and cavalier disregard for common practice and the patient's welfare.

What we have is a system of legal shakedown by the plaintiff's lawyers. Don't like how things turned out? It must be somebody's fault. Call us and we will get you (and us) lots of money. It doesn't matter if they didn't do anything wrong. We will get you the cash. That may sound a little harsh, but it's the way I feel.

I went through one (yes only one) malpractice suit. (My wrong site surgery was an obvious mistake, and we compensated that patient before any actual suit was filed.) Another woman was a long-time patient, who I thought I had a good long-term relationship with. But she had a complication after an arthroscopic knee surgery called reflex sympathetic dystrophy syndrome (RSD) (can happen to anyone after an injury or surgery) and was left with some residual pain and dysfunction. To this day, I don't think I did anything wrong. But two weeks before the statute of limitations ran out, her attorneys filed a malpractice suit against me. I'm sure that, since she was having some residual trouble, someone got in her ear and said, "You can get some money for this." So off we go.

Very long story short, (over five years and many sleepless nights on my part), my attorney, my insurance company, and I agreed to give them a settlement. That was more than I wanted to give them. I wanted to fight it all the way and give them nothing because I didn't do anything wrong! But, it was far less than it would have cost to defend it in court.

We agreed to a payoff without any admission of wrongdoing or blame being assigned to me (which I wanted) and money for them (which is what they wanted). It was a payoff to make them go away. Very disillusioning.

But the worst is the fact that every day (and night), it dominates almost your every thought. You can't get it out of your mind. It's always there. You obsess over it. You can see why people settle just to get it gone so it doesn't kill you with worry and anger. And the plaintiff's lawyers know this. In my case, the head of the law firm said, under oath in the mediation, "We are going to go after everything you have, Dr. Chase. Your home, your car, everything." The emotional toll it takes is tremendous.

Patients with No Incentive to Get Better

One of the hardest things we deal with is patients who don't want to get better. How is that, you say? Who doesn't want to get better? Lots of people. The common denominator is when they have a secondary gain for not improving. It might be easily recognizable. Or, It may be very hidden. Here are a few reasons why they might not want to get well.

1. Legal. They have a lawsuit against somebody and if they get better, they (and their attorneys) won't get any money. Old saying: "Your lawyer doesn't want you to get better."

2. Workers' Compensation (WC). If they get better, they have to go back to the job they didn't like. It is well documented that the likelihood of a WC patient not improving is directly related to how unhappy they were with their job before the injury. We have a term called WC disease. They have more pain, they can never go back to work (or it takes forever), and they have a lawyer.

3. Both 1 and 2. They are the worst.

Hidden Agendas

As an orthopaedic surgeon, I never cease to be amazed at how many different hidden agendas can masquerade as the innocuous complaint of knee pain. Don't you wish you had a little monitor on the patient's forehead that actually said why they were really in your office? It would make treating them much easier if you could actually identify the real reason they are there. The following is a list of reasons why a patient may be seeing you with the same chief complaint. This list is certainly not all inclusive.

Justifiable Reasons:

- This really hurts and I am here to get it fixed so I can return to normal activities. (This is what we hope every patient is there for.)

- This really hurts. How long will I have to be out of work? (Usually farmers or people depending on their own efforts for their living.)

- I am here to make sure it isn't serious or if I should be doing something different.

- This hurts and I will probably have to live with it, but what are my options?

- I think I'm fine, but my _____ (family member) made me come in to make sure it was not something serious.

Suspect Reasons

- I am here because I am not happy with my life and I need something to focus on.

- I am here because I want somebody to talk to.

- I am here because I don't like my job and I am trying to find a way to get out of it and still be paid.

- I am here because my lawyer told me I need a doctor to say what my problem is, who caused it and to fill out forms and go to depositions and maybe a trial.

- I am here because I want to get a lot of money for my pain and suffering.

- I am here because if I can get you to operate on me and I don't do well, then I can sue you and make a lot of money for me and my attorney for my pain and suffering.

- I am here because this hurts and I want narcotics.

- I am here because this chief complaint is all made up and I want narcotics.

- I am here because I don't like the looks of this part of my body. (Orthopaedists don't usually do cosmetic surgery.)

- I am here because I need you to fill out prescriptions.

- I am here because I need you to fill out insurance forms.

- I am here because I need you to give me a disabled parking permit because I don't like to walk so far to go shopping.

- Everybody I have been to says they cannot find anything wrong, but I hope you can.

- I am here because everybody I have been to says I have a problem but they can't help me.

- I am here because I need you to change your dictation because the way it is worded does not fit my needs.

- I am here because my child is terrible at sports and there must be something medically wrong with him.

- I am here because I am running 90 miles a week and can't figure out why my legs hurt.

- There is nothing wrong with me, but I would like to sell you some ___ (insurance, investments, etc.)

Patients don't usually announce these reasons, but it eventually becomes clear what their motives are. These are all real. You can't make this stuff up!

If we actually knew the real reason our patients are seeing us, it would help us better address the problem and we could spend less time spinning our wheels working up something that isn't addressing their hidden agenda.

Chronically Tired for 40 Years

Doctors have to get very good at functioning chronically tired. Because you always are. It started in college, studying late and getting up early for labs. Same for the first two years in medical school. Then comes clinical work and when you are working 60-100 hours per week, you are sleep deprived. After residency, it gets better, somewhat. You are still on call. And you are still working 60 hours a week.

I spent my whole career chronically tired. In the afternoon, I would sit down to read (charts, medical articles, books, newspapers or magazines) and I would immediately fall into apid eye movement (REM) sleep and dream. How do I know? I'm retired now. I wake up when I wake up and I don't fall asleep during the day. Such a joy.

Not Knowing

You have to get comfortable (although I'm not sure you ever really are) with sometimes not knowing what is going on with your patient. Not comfortable for you, or them. But sometimes you can't. Don't beat yourself up, take it home with you, stew over it and drive yourself crazy. Learn to say, "I did the best I could" and come back to fight another day. And even when you are able to accomplish this, there will still be times you go home or are in the car or are trying to sleep and it dominates your mind. An internal medicine resident I had in medical school had the best advice on this. "You may not always know what your patient has. But you need to know what he doesn't have."

Failure

Most people have some fear of failure. Doctors are very good at that. It starts in the days of pre-med when they were so paranoid that they wouldn't get into medical school. When you get in, it's not so much exhilaration as it is relief that you didn't fail.

You can fail at patients. Every time you see a patient, it's like checking your scores on the bulletin board outside the Chemistry department to see if you got an A or a C or if you failed.

It's certainly not all on you if your patients aren't doing well, but guilt makes it seem like it is.

You can fail at the business side of your practice. Not enough patients to cover your costs. Too much overhead. Risks taken with capital expenditures. Staff problems. Poor hires and interpersonal problems. If you have a small practice, you are the human resources (HR) manager, something you were never trained to do. Doctors are intelligent people, but that doesn't always translate into smart business decisions.

You can fail at your investments. When I was interviewing, I took my contract to an attorney and he looked at it and said, "This contract is fine. But, let me give you some advice that will make the $200 you just paid me worth it. Never take investment advice from a doctor!"

Taking Things Personally

People you operate on sometimes don't do well or have complications. It's very disappointing. It is hard not to take it personally and ask, "What did I do wrong? I call it Doctor Catholic guilt. Rightly or wrongly, we take it very personally.

Sometimes you can predict outcomes. There are some people you get done with and say, "I never should have operated on them." But sometimes those same people you had reservations about do great and you think, "What was I worried about?" And then there are people you would have predicted would have no trouble, but they struggle mightily. The question is, is it temporary and you just have to wait it out or will they be permanently unhappy?

You Are Responsible for People's Inaction

Sounds weird, but if you tell a patient they need to do something, even if you're good about documenting it, and they are noncompliant and don't do what you told them, you can be held responsible for and sued for them having a big problem later. "If it was really important," says the lawyer, "You should have repeatedly attempted to contact them and made sure they got this terrible problem under treatment. It is now your fault, Doctor, that this patient has cancer spread all over their body." And the case will not be thrown out! Doesn't seem right, does it? Where is the concept of personal responsibility?

One of the more common reasons doctors get behind is too much information. Every doctor's nightmare is seeing a patient that comes in with reams of information from "the internet" and they want to discuss with you everything they have read. Or, they have pages of questions, single spaced, that they are going to ask you. These people either have obsessive compulsive disorder (OCD) or are engineers. Maybe both. It's good that patients read and become educated. But there are degrees.

I used to tell my patients "The Internet is information without perspective. It's my job to give you that perspective. Don't get hung up on the minutiae. Focus on the big picture."

Family Leaves During Surgery

After surgery, I like to go out and personally talk with the family to let them know how things went. Not call. Not give the job to someone else. One of my pet peeves was when there was no family there to talk to, despite the nurses telling them not to leave. What more important things do you have to do than to talk with the doctor and find out how the surgery went for your family member?

They would leave to go lunch. They would leave to go shopping. They would run errands. If their child was being operated on, it was a great time to leave. Babysitting they didn't have to pay for. And this was not rare. I would say 20% of the time.

Every Day Fears

Every day you are in fear of what might come in the door. Infections are always a problem. Patients think, "Infection, he'll just put me on oral antibiotics and it will all be fine." Not so. They frequently need urgent surgery to wash out the infection, admission to hospital and intravenous (IV) antibiotics for weeks. If it is a total joint, it can be an unmitigated disaster. They may need their joint replacement removed, multiple surgeries with antibiotics and they are frequently never as good as they were before the infection.

There are other complications. Some you anticipate can happen. If there's too much bleeding, they can die. Nerve damage can occur in any of our surgeries, including cutting a nerve you can't see because of a scar. It is sometimes anticipated and you tell them about the possibility, but it doesn't make it any easier when it happens. Some are bizarre and happen totally out of the blue with no obvious reason. But, there they are.

Everybody we see with a diagnosis that is not really obvious (and some where it is), we are worried about missing something. A tumor, an infection, an impending spinal cord damage, something. Because we have all heard stories of people who go to multiple doctors, nobody can find anything, they are told that they are crazy and then some other smart doctor swoops in and makes the brilliant diagnosis saving their life and if they had stayed with Dr. Chase, they would be dead now. A little dramatic, but we fear it.

You Have to Make Quick Decisions

We know that. Emergencies are part of the job. What you may not realize is, you will be judged later and held to the standards with 20-20 hindsight. Malpractice attorneys and their hired "experts" comfortably pick and choose medical literature that supports their case that you were negligent while you were trying to do the best you could under trying emergency circumstances.

You Have to Be the Bad Guy a Lot

We have to be the bad guy a lot. We have to say no. No to requests for handicap parking stickers in perfectly healthy people. No to surgery on crazy people. No to surgery in the morbidly obese. No to narcotics. No to their insistence that they can't go back to work. No to their lawyer's insistence that their back pain (and every other malady they can think of) is not caused by their original knee injury and it's all not connected. No, they aren't totally disabled from fibromyalgia.

We have to tell people we can't find anything wrong with them. We have to tell people they have something terrible. Cancer. Torn ligaments and they can't play their sport their senior season. Tell them we can't fix their problem so they can walk their daughter down the aisle at their wedding. No wonder you see patients leave the office crying or storming out and calling us every name in the book. Sometimes you just have to say no. Joe

Tutorino once said, "The short answer is no. The long answer is "Hell no."

Curbside Consults

A very common thing is that other doctors, friends, family, and neighbors pull you aside and say "I have this …" and they want you to tell them it's okay, or what you have or how you should treat it. Beware. You can't win. You think you are trying to do them a favor and you aren't. I always said, "When a patient comes in, we do a real evaluation and we don't know them from Adam. Why would I do a half-baked evaluation with a much poorer chance of actually being right for people I know and love?"

The right answer is to tell them, "Make an appointment so I can get all the right information and do a proper job." Most reasonable people understand and do so. The jerks who are just trying to get free advice (it's worth what you pay for it) get mad and that's okay.

Best story about this was a man I'll call Sam. Sam had this pain in the side of his hip. Almost always bursitis. His best friend and golf partner, who happened to be an Orthopaedist, had been telling him for months to ice it, use Motrin, and even gave him a cortisone injection. All to no avail. But it wasn't bad until Sam woke up one morning and urinated gross blood from his bladder. Long story short, the hip pain was the presenting symptom of metastatic renal cancer to his femur. If he had been a regular patient in the office, the doctor would have taken an x-ray and made a diagnosis right away. Of course, the die was cast when the cancer got to the bone, so Sam had no chance. Both he and his friend felt terrible!

This leads to the observation that doctors' families get the worst care. Because of friendships like the story above, often their symptoms just aren't taken seriously. I even sent my soccer player daughter, Anna, back into a game with a fractured wrist ("Soccer players don't use their hands. Get back in there.") Well, the bone wasn't sticking through the skin!

Marian's Tonsillectomy

The old axiom that, "Bad things happen to doctors, doctor's wives and nurses" was something I learned early in my career. My wife, Marian, had a tonsillectomy when I was a resident. (We both worked at that hospital). In the recovery room, many friends came in to check on her. Several of them were anesthesiologists and said to her, "Are you having pain? Here, let me get you some morphine." She got groggier and groggier and I said, "We have got to get you out of here before somebody kills you with all this kindness."

Direct to Consumer Advertising

I am not a fan of this. It causes us in the office to spend our time explaining why this expensive medicine with a million side effects is entirely inappropriate for this patient or that what I prescribed for them is better and less expensive.

We get information like The Medical Letter that has unbiased, evidence-based drug reviews and is a great resource for deciding which medicines to use. Also, don't get your information from reps. They are the ultimate in bias.

"YOU WHAT?" Patient Moments

You would not believe what we deal with sometimes with patients. I tried very hard to explain things to people in detail, and if I didn't quite give them all they needed, I also tried very hard to answer their questions. But, sometimes You Just Can't Win. Anybody that deals with the public knows this. There are just some people that defy logic and can't be made happy no matter what you do.

Ultimate Insult to a Doctor

I scheduled a lady for an arthroscopic surgery for a meniscus tear in her knee. She had an incidental Baker's cyst in the back of her knee, which is quite common. The principal is to treat the underlying source of the problem, the meniscus tear, and the Bakers cyst (usually not a source of any of the pain) will diminish or disappear on its own. I have never excised or even drained a Bakers' cyst at surgery in 34 years because it is almost universally not a problem later. Why take risks of blood vessels or nerve damage for something that is not a problem?

I specifically told her this when discussing the surgery in the office, as well as later. In response to her phone call, I called her (and documented it in the chart) to explain that we don't remove or even drain Bakers' cysts at the time of surgery due to the risk of damaging large nerves and blood vessels in the back of the knee where the cyst is. We went ahead with the surgery without complications and she was getting better.

She later wrote a letter to our "marketing department" (really?) to "bring to someone's attention" my substandard care for not draining the Bakers cyst at the time of the surgery. She stated that she "talked to several people" (didn't say who or what their background was) who said it is not uncommon to drain them at the time of the surgery.

She also said, "It was suggested to her that Dr. Chase was trying to generate another procedure and its fees and that is why he didn't drain it then. She just wanted to let someone know."

I explained the situation to her multiple times and she had the audacity to insinuate my care was inadequate and that I was trying to make more money off her. She is also the person who will trash me to ten of her friends and fill out bad evaluation forms on social media and other online reviews.

Pee on the Floor

People sometimes get upset at what we have to tell them. Sometimes they cry and shed tears and you give them Kleenex to soak up their tears. Sometimes you have to soak up other stuff.

One adult woman saw me for her knee and didn't like what I had to tell her. I did not feel she had good indications for surgery and I told her that I thought surgery would not help her. (This was the honest but sometimes evasive explanation I gave people when I thought they were not a good candidate for surgery, mostly because of their personality. I wasn't saying that they didn't have a problem. I was saying that surgery with me was never going to happen.)

She of course started crying, which was not uncommon. I hate it, but it happens. But then, she started throwing a tantrum. Now, she was not four, she was 24. After a while, she laid down on the floor to continue throwing her tantrum, (which only proved me right not to operate on her), and at that point, there was no rational dealing with her. She left, ranting about how awful I was to everyone in the waiting room. Keyunna, my assistant, went into the room to clean up for the next patient and found a puddle on the floor where she had been laying down. It was yellow and it smelled like, yes, urine! This was voluntary rage induced incontinence. A new one for me.

HIV Patient Wouldn't Tell Us

This one is actually scary. A man came in with a locked knee, an urgent problem, and we added him on for surgery. There was no mention of any medical problems or medications on his medical history form. When the pre-op nurses at the surgery center were preparing his chart, they noticed his medications from the pharmacy included antiviral meds for human immunodeficiency virus (HIV) AIDS!

If you don't give us accurate information about all your medical conditions, we can make decisions that can harm you or even kill you!

When they asked him about it, he said, "I don't have to tell you that!" It's true, there are laws meant to protect people who are HIV+ from discrimination. We are not allowed to deny a patient treatment if they have AIDS-HIV because it is a "Protected Condition." But, who's protecting us? This guy is allowed to lie to us about relevant medical conditions that could compromise his care and put me and my operative staff at risk for contracting a deadly disease in surgery?! Doesn't seem right, does it?

Mike on Call

My friend Mike MacMillan had the worst. He was asleep in his bed at home at midnight. It's July and all the new interns are starting. His beeper goes off (this was a long time ago). He calls the emergency room and the surgical intern breathlessly gasps, "Dr. MacMillan! Big Accident! Broken bones for sure!" Then he hangs up the phone.

What are you supposed to do with that? The patient just got to the ER and no workup has even started, so there is no point in rushing in. They are not even sure you will be needed. But you can't go back to sleep after that call. Your mind immediately starts racing with the myriad of possibilities, all of which will keep you up all night. You don't know when that call will come in, but it will. Usually, just as you are starting to drift off to sleep.

Sights and Smells

Some people think it is glamorous to be a doctor. They have nice houses. They drive nice cars. They seem to have some prestige. Let me tell you how glamorous it can be.

I was a junior resident in Orthopaedics at the Veterans (VA) hospital and we had just fixed a hip fracture for an older veteran. As the junior resident, I would get all the calls for patients on the Orthopaedic floor. About 1 am, I got a call from the nurses about this gentleman whose abdomen was getting progressively larger and larger. I asked them to get some tests and x-rays and I would be in shortly, as I took the call from home.

When I saw him, it looked like his belly was going to blow up! He wasn't in a lot of distress, but if it got much larger, his bowel could rupture. It turns out he had something called Ogilvies syndrome where the bowel goes into paralysis without actually getting obstructed. The treatment is a nasogastric tube into the stomach from up top and a rectal tube from below to decompress the bowel while it recovers and they usually get better with some time.

While writing my notes, the nurses kept coming up to me and telling me the rectal tube keeps getting blocked with feces and can't decompress all the air in the bowel. So, here is my conundrum. I could go home, get calls every half hour about the tube getting blocked, the bowel may not decompress and he could get much worse or even die! Or, I could just make sure that air got out.

So, we rolled him on his side and I put an index finger from each hand in his rectum and opened the anus with the hoped for rush of air (better known as a fart!) coming right at my face! I sat there for about a half an hour while getting a steady fart in my face, with the expected smell accompanying it!

His bowel quickly decompressed and I got to go home and sleep without getting further calls about him the rest of the night. Not quite what I was planning on when I went into Orthopaedics, but you gotta do what you gotta do!

PART 2

YOUR REWARDS

CHAPTER 10

MY "I WHAT?" MOMENT

After reading the last two chapters, you may wonder, "Why would anyone want to do this?" This chapter is why.

Dr. William Enneking, one of our esteemed faculty at the University of Florida Medical School, was an internationally renowned orthopaedic surgeon. He invented a classification of sarcomas and wrote a seminal book on musculoskeletal orthopaedic tumors.

He inspired fear in established orthopaedic surgeons all over the country if he was going to question them. In my mind, he embodied the Socratic method. I never got the impression that he was trying to make us look stupid, he was trying to push us to learn. While he was pretty brutal with other orthopaedic surgeons, with his own residents, he was fair, but he was tough. So much so that, you better not have a thin skin.

At the end of my residency, there was a big end of year dinner. Nobody in orthopaedics would believe this, but Dr. Enneking wrote a poem about me and my fellow resident Mike MacMillan and he actually read it at the dinner! It was so out of character for him to do something like that and that's why it meant so much to me. This is a reprint of that poem:

Poem from Enneking:

They went for six
Long way to go
John was blonde
With eyes so blue
While Mike was dark
And so strong too
They went for six
Some pain, some woe

Mike so bright, ideas so new
John so steady, a rock so true
They went for six
They started slow
But look at them now
Look at them go
Wish I were there
I want you to know
You went for six
And gave us a glow
So John and Mike
And Mike and John
All of our best wishes
To carry on
Welcome aboard
Join the crew
And know how proud
We are of you
WFE (William Fisher Enneking)

My Retirement Announcement

The last year of my practice was miserable. But once I made that announcement in January 2020, everything was better. Everything. I made plans to retire March 31st. I had kept a list of people who were thinking about surgery and called them. I didn't want them to call and have them be told "He's gone." I wanted them to hear it from me. Then, a funny thing happened.

Once that announcement went out, I began to receive some remarkable, wonderful feedback!

First, I wanted to get all my surgeries done and people well on their way to recovery before retiring. Contrary to what I thought would happen (that people would get mad and claim I was abandoning them), I had a number of people say, "Well, I want you to do my surgery, so let's get it scheduled."

I set February 15th as my last day and I did eight surgeries that day. So much for slowing down on the way out! A sweet young woman I had operated on before came in after I had stopped scheduling surgery and broke into tears when I told her I couldn't schedule because there wasn't enough time to do proper follow up. She said, "I don't care. I want you to do it." So, I did her arthroscopy February 27th and she did fine. I got the nicest card from her that said, in part, "I am so thankful for your knowledge and unbeatable level of compassion. I will always be thankful for you. ~Your last surgical patient."

As the weeks went on and I saw more and more people in the office, my feedback got better and better. Some people already knew and wanted to come in and say goodbye and thank you. One started crying and said, "Who is going to take care of me and my family?" Some came in and said, "I want you to tell me who I should see if you aren't going to be here anymore." It was very emotional for me, as well!

Connection

What this showed to me was how incredibly fortunate we are in this business to make such a strong connection with people. There were people who I had been seeing for over 30 years. With some of them, I feel like I have made a friend. One family, I treated all of them at one time or another, did a research project with one of their daughters, and we still keep in touch with

Christmas cards. Another family, I did ACL surgery on both the son then the father. That doesn't happen often.

One patient became my idol. He was a few years older than me and was a teacher and track coach and still was pole vaulting after 30 years. (I pole vaulted as a young man and it was my greatest thrill in all the sports I did. We had an instant bond.) I did surgery on him that was only supposed to last for five to ten years. He kept pole vaulting through the years and came and saw me for maintenance and treatments. It was fun to help keep him going. He finally came to me for advice on who to do his knee replacement so he could keep vaulting. I had stopped doing them a few years earlier. Now, he is still pole vaulting after his knee replacement! My idol. He invited me to come see his home pole vaulting setup and he and his wife welcomed my granddaughter (only three years old) when I brought her with me.

Trust

These stories are not typical. But what is very common, and I was always amazed by (and still am), was the trust that people placed in us as surgeons. They let us cut them (and their children) open with sharp knives, sometimes without knowing us or much about us or for not very long. That goes to the reputation of our group's medical abilities early in our careers and then our individual reputations after we had been around long enough to get a reputation.

Taking Care of Nice People

The thing I liked the absolute most about my career was the opportunity to take care of nice people!!! These people have a smile on their face from the minute you meet them. They are honest about their problem, understanding of the options, compliant with instructions, appreciative when things go well, understanding when they don't. You see them on the schedule and you smile. They tell their equally nice friends about you and that's how you build up a good practice. That's fun.

Nice people appreciate your honesty and integrity. These are the people you hope you have a few extra minutes for when you aren't an hour behind because you just like talking with them. And not necessarily about their medical problem. If you have a few minutes, you can learn some really interesting things about people. It makes for a more interesting day.

That is my definition of a successful practice, which may be at odds with the conventional interpretation (lucrative).

What This Career Gives You

A Good Living

You can make a good living in a career in medicine. If you want to be filthy rich, you might choose another career. You have to work too hard when your income is almost solely dependent on your individual effort.

Fix It!

What's really nice about orthopaedics is you can fix things. Fix a fracture, repair a tendon rupture or laceration. You can take a really messed up extremity, put things in the right position, and they can heal and be absolutely as good as new. It doesn't happen every time, but at least it's possible. Even if you can't "Fix it," you can frequently reconstruct it and people can get back to unlimited activity. So cool!

There are plenty of problems that can't be made whole. It's your responsibility to give people what I call realistic hope, especially when they see all those people that are back to 100% and question why they aren't. That is the realistic expectations part.

I used to do ACL reconstructions on high school kids. On their last visit, when I turned them loose to unlimited activity, I would tell them, "Send me your high school soccer (or basketball or or lacrosse) schedule. I would then pick a game when I didn't have another commitment that night and go to their game and sit with their parents. They appreciated it and I enjoyed immensely seeing them get back to what they wanted to do. Very cool!

You can reassure people even if you don't do anything. There are things you can't fix. There are things you can do nothing at all for. There are things you have no earthly idea what it is. And we are uncomfortable with that. We want to fix it but sometimes, the only thing you can do is listen. And sometimes, that is as valuable as anything else, although we don't feel like it. We feel like we are failures, but if you just spend a little time listening (that would imply you have that time), you can provide a great service to the patient and it's just what they need.

Some of my most loyal patients are those that I could do nothing for at all. I'd see people and ask who sent you to see us and it would be one of those unsuccessful patients who sent them and I would be dumbfounded. Sometimes out of the blue people tell you how pleased or grateful they are. Even if you didn't think you did anything special. It was very gratifying.

Helping Neighbors and Friends

One of the great things about this career is you can help your neighbors and friends with something that is very important to them just by talking to them on the phone. "I just wrenched my knee. Should I go to the ER?" "My Dad is having a hip replacement and we are really worried about it?"

Even non orthopaedic stuff, we still know more than they do. Just a conversation on the phone can give them immense comfort that they shouldn't be doing something else. I would get those calls all the time and I didn't mind. Most people just wanted some advice about what direction to go. We frequently told our daughters soccer teammates or my basketball friends to come over to the house and I would check them and point them in the right direction. One of our couches was even called the examination couch.

On my last day in surgery, my youngest daughter, Anna, unbeknownst to me, had put out a Facebook message asking people who I had impacted to "Help me send him off into retirement with memories of a career that made a difference." Here are some of those posts:

Jamee: Congratulations!! He made an impact on me. I still remember the days he let me follow him before I went to med school. He walked me through his cases and let me see some of his OR cases. I hadn't had much exposure to medicine yet and I identify this time shadowing him as some of the first times I knew I really wanted to be a doc.

Alice: May he enjoy a wonderful retirement! He definitely made an impact in our house. My husband is in Colorado skiing at this very moment after knee surgery one year ago. Thank you Dr. Chase!

Mari: Dr. Chase is the best! Aside from him being so kind and funny when I hung out with Sarah, I will always remember going to him in high school when I tore my ACL. I think we did a couch consultation because I tore my ACL during a weekend soccer tournament, but I'm sure we also did an official office visit before my surgery.

Magdalena: Enjoy every day of your well-deserved retirement Dr. Chase!! It was my honor to work with you! I miss you already, my friend…

Stacy: I will also never forget what he did for our family when my Dad was in the cardiac ICU. It was amazing to have a family friend help us translate what was really happening

Madeline: Remember when under anesthesia post-surgery, I told all his nurses that he cheats at Taboo?

Mishri: I have so much to say. Your Dad is the reason my Mom can walk so effortlessly and for long distances. It was needed after she had a heart attack five years later and needed to get into better shape. She lost 30 pounds.

Very, very few friends abused us and tried to get treated for nothing. A very cool thing to do for the people you care about.

Meet Some Incredible People

As in any field, you get to meet and know some incredible people you work with. In our orthopaedic office, we had many hard-working dedicated people who, by doing their jobs well, allowed us to do our jobs well. Doctors are not easy to work for.

They are almost always Type A, frequently impatient and there are high expectations. There are not a lot of thank you's. They had to get their satisfaction from knowing they did a good job because they did not get a lot of positive reinforcement. I was there for 34 years and we had GG of all trades and my office manager Meredith who had been there for 45 years! That's a long time in one place. You don't see that much anymore.

We had some great physician assistants (PAs) and nurse practitioners (NPs). They weren't surgeons and didn't try to be doctors. Some were even so thorough and pleasant that the patients wanted to see them, rather than the doctors.

I know I have said this, but it bears repeating. I considered the people I worked with in the operating rooms some of the finest people I have had the pleasure to get to know. They had difficult hours and sometimes very demanding conditions to work in, especially with all the challenging surgeons they had to deal with. They were almost always unfailingly pleasant and, if you weren't terrible to them, as helpful and respectful as they could be. These people worked very hard with high stress from being in surgery (the surgery itself or from the surgeons) and taking care of the patient's safety (the circulating registered nurse's (RN's) main job). They got very little thanks and lots of crap.

You get the pleasure of accomplishing something useful working with people you like. You rotate with different people in your room each day. So you get to know, pretty well, a number of different people. This group includes the orderlies, CRNAs and anesthesiologists. It's interesting that the patients get good exposure to the people in the check in area, the pre-op area and the recovery room. Their view of their experience is dependent on these groups of people. Very important! But they don't get any exposure that they remember (because of medication or they are under anesthesia) to the people who take care of them in surgery itself.

Physical Therapists

Speaking of incredible people… I hold a special place for our therapists. The therapists I worked with are some of the most professional and competent health care professionals I know. All of us depended on the physical therapists and the hand surgeons were especially dependent on the occupational therapists. And that's a good word: dependent. We all know we can do a technically proficient surgery and if the therapy is poor (or worse, nonexistent), the eventual results can be abysmal. I always said "We, as orthopedists, are better at structural things and the therapists are better at dynamic things."

I was very fortunate throughout the years to have some great therapists to work with and in recent years, have them be on the same floor where we could confer and discuss a difficult patient. (Difficult can be meant in lots of ways.) A good therapist is like a good parent. If they are too nice they are not doing their job. Their job is to push people. That's how these problems get better and a great therapist finds a way to get that done and have the patient still love them.

They had to be experts in anatomy and kinetics, but they also had to be psychologists as well, dealing with many people who were "difficult." Aside from their qualifications and skill, they were just great people! Always professional, they were very solid and unpretentious. No divas here. And they are the ones you want to ask, "What doctor should I have do my surgery?" They see all our patients and know whose patients fly through and whose routinely struggle.

Teaching

Another reward of a long career is the opportunity to teach. I enjoy it and I care enough to want to do it well. That is what this book is turning out to be as I write it. My treatise on how to be a good doctor. That wasn't how it started out. What I don't want is to be presumptuous, preachy and boring. Hopefully, I've succeeded.

High School Team Doctor

In 1989, I was called at the last minute to help bail out Roger Mosure, a local high school trainer, when his team physician bailed on him the day before doing that high school's pre-participation physicals for the students. We got along well and that started my 30 years of being the team physician for our office's neighborhood public high school, which I enjoyed immensely.

It was a natural connection to the community. I met lots of teachers and coaches. And as I aged, it kept my entire practice from becoming as old as I was with the infusion of high school students for patients every year.

I enjoyed this even more than taking care of a pro team, which I also did. High school students usually listen to your recommendations and the job is different than it was for pro athletes. With the pros, you give them information and they make decisions about their injury and career. With high school kids, you have a different job: to actually think about their long-term health. You have to protect student athletes from themselves and occasionally the coaches, but most often their parents who have a great emotional need to get their kid back to their sport.

My particular privilege was getting to know and work with a great group of athletic trainers. These people are the hardest working, with the longest hours, with very little recognition and they have great impact on the health of their athletes from athletic injuries.

And we had a great time. Hours on a football field with surprisingly few major injuries gives you lots of time to get to know these, usually, great people. We all had a good cooperative working relationship trying to help the kids avoid major injury, to rehab properly when they did get injured, and to heal.

Mission Work

One of the more memorable and impactful things I have had the opportunity to do as an orthopaedic surgeon is mission work. I don't know why, but I felt the need in the early 1990s to go on a surgical mission trip to the Dominican Republic where our Diocese has a sister mission in the town of San Juan de la Maguana. Our family was young and I give my wife Marian great credit and thanks for letting me gallivant off to a foreign country for a week, leaving her to manage three young kids by herself.

At first, I was terrified. I was afraid for my health. I was afraid for my life. I didn't know if I could eat the food, so I took 21 power Bars to keep me alive. But it turned out to be a fabulous experience. I loved it and it was very worthwhile and fulfilling for me to do.

I worked really hard for a week, did a whole bunch of incredible surgeries that we would never do here. We would never even see those kinds of problems here. I call it the long-term consequences of untreated orthopaedic disease. People there had just never been attended to.

When I saw the facilities and equipment, I was horrified. But I calmed down when someone told me, "It may not be what you are used to, but it is the best that these people have. Whatever you do will be better than if you never came." So, I jumped in and we worked very hard. I saw unbelievable things; the results of untreated orthopaedic disease and trauma. It was amazing to see what we could do there and to know, it really does make a difference. We never see problems this advanced in the U.S.

To my amazement, I had a wonderful and astonishing time. I met great people helping out and made a lifelong friend in the woman who had the misfortune of being assigned to me as my interpreter, Beatrice Ginebra, who we all called "Bea." Bea is originally from the Dominican Republic, but has lived in the States for most of her life. I saw joy and happiness in people who had absolutely nothing, but were much happier than many people in the U.S. who have everything they need and want.

As part of this mission trip, I was introduced to a boy named Roberto who suffered from severe knee deformities that forced him to walk on all fours. My interpreter, Bea, and I looked at him and said, we can't do anything for him here, but why don't we see if we can bring him back to the United States and do surgery there that might help him. Roberto's nickname was "Horse Boy" because he walked like a horse.

I talked to the hospital and got them to let us do the surgery. Then, I talked to the prosthesis company and got them to donate the prostheses. What we did was, amputate both his legs. Bea kept him in her house for four months. I did his surgery and supervised his rehabilitation and got him his prostheses. His big goal was to learn to dance.

An unexpected part of this story is that Life Magazine had been wanting to do an article about someone going through an amputation from start to finish. They had talked to this prosthesis company and when I approached them about donating the prostheses, they said, this is exactly what Life Magazine was looking for. They contacted me and asked if I would be willing to be involved. I reluctantly said, yes. I did not want them to make a spectacle of this boy. I did not want him to be portrayed as a freak with a gawking media frenzy. And I was perfectly willing to let the whole thing go under the radar. But I also thought it was a good story, if they did it professionally.

Then, Life contacted the ABC TV show 20/20 and they got involved. I again reluctantly agreed to have them onboard. Fortunately, they did a great job. They were unobtrusive, and did not get in the way. They handled everything very professionally. The photographer and reporter from Life Magazine, plus the 20/20 correspondents and their cameraman were all involved from start to finish. It appeared on 20/20 and also in Life Magazine in 1998. When my sister Abby saw the 20/20 show, the first thing she did was call me up and say, "They made you look much better than you are!" Leave it to sisters to keep you humble.

Soon after, there was a big hurricane and Roberto's home got flooded. He barely got out of there with his prostheses. So, we went back and tried to help him. Our goal was to get him to be independent, which he achieved. He was able to walk like a human, rather than like a dog.

There's obviously a lot more to this story. But if you find yourself feeling unfulfilled, or you just have a desire to contribute to something outside your own little world, consider finding a group or a place where you can serve others. It will change your life.

Working with a Professional Team

In 1989, the Orlando Magic was a brand new NBA team and my orthopaedic group got the contract to take care of them. I wasn't the main guy, there were four of us. But, I would cover a lot. I attended and worked about 25% of their games as the team physician. I got to know most of the players, and some of them knew who I was. I did it for nine years and it was a great experience. I loved it.

For three or four years, I would go out on road trips with them. I got to go to the Boston Gardens and Chicago Stadium. I got to see Larry Bird and Michael Jordan play live. The whole thing was fabulous! I love basketball. So, for me to be able to do that was really thrilling. As far as I was concerned, it ended too soon.

As far as the actual care goes, I would definitely prefer to take care of high school kids because they actually listen to you. Their parents listen to you, usually. There is a different focus. As a doctor, I like to consider their long-term health in my recommendations. With professionals, we can only give them the information. Then, they make the decision whether they go back to playing or not. What's more important, their long-term health or the playoffs coming up? They want to make that decision. So, it's just a different focus. It was a great opportunity and one of my rewards for those early delayed gratification years we talked about.

Retirement Party

The surgery center where I worked and felt closest to the people there gave me a "Retirement Party." When there is an event (like birthdays or retirements), somebody gets a card and everybody writes a couple of words on it. There is not much room on a store-bought card. What was most significant to me was, somebody put out some of the blank white cards that we used to post the surgeries on the main board and said, "Leave Dr. Chase a note if you want."

I was amazed that during a busy surgical day, people would actually take the time to write something. Here are some of those cards, all from RN's:

Brenda: "Thank you for always remembering my name. It always meant so much to me that you remembered it right away."

Angie: "We will miss you and you will definitely leave a hole that will be hard to fill. You have been a pleasure to work with for many reasons, but not the least is your kindness."

Ethel: "When I was hired in June 2000, we were introduced in the hallway. Two and a half weeks later, on my first day, we ran into each other in the lounge and you greeted me by my first name. I was so impressed, especially since my last job was ten years full time and when I left, several doctors still had no idea of my name. You will always be remembered for your attentiveness, humor, kindness, and real concern for excellent patient care."

Amy: "You have taught me so much about what it means to be kindhearted and sincere. Gonna miss you around here something fierce. You always treated us the very best."

Lynette "You always made me feel like a competent, important member of the team. Thank you for allowing me the time to eat lunch when you arrived for your cases. It was an honor to have worked with you."

I also got a nice message from Michelle, one of our NP's who said, "I will always tell others what a huge mentor you were for me when I first began in Ortho. I find many "Chase-isms" in my routine office life and I was so fortunate to have you steer me along. I haven't seen you for a while, so I can't say your retirement will leave a huge void in my day to day. However, I'm already hearing patients tell me how much they will miss you. Your absence will be quite a loss for all of us left behind and for those who won't receive your guidance in the future."

My retirement party was the culmination and affirmation that I had done things the right way. I got to experience the rewards of my own top three pieces of advice: Treat people decently. Take good care of your patients by being conscientious and responsible. And, enjoy yourself along the way.

PART 3

YOUR LIFE

CHAPTER 11
SETTING YOUR STANDARDS

The Big Question

The big question for me starting out was: "Am I doing the Right Thing?" This question is the one you ask yourself, inside your own mind.

AM I DOING THE RIGHT THING?

I was always asking myself this question. Sub-questions to this are:

"Am I missing anything?" (This is for you. You always think this.)

"Did I screw up?" (This is usually in fear of lawsuits.)

This is a struggle, but it affects how you sleep at night. You think about these things with every patient, every day! Your decisions are what make you a success or a failure, just like a quarterback or a point guard.

Before you can answer, "Am I doing the Right Thing?" you have to decide, "What is the Right Thing?" You make that decision based on your core principles. This will be different for everybody as we all arrange our priorities differently. For me, it's important to get the Right Things in order.

Your core principles are what determine your standards. Take some time to figure out what your standards are and what they mean to you. Mine were established by my family and in Iowa, the place I grew up.

Be Conscientious and Responsible

Know your stuff. You have to know your stuff. That means keeping up with your reading. Everybody is up to date when they finish their residency, but it is hard to keep up with your reading (Journals, new research) with all your other demands in practice. It takes real effort, which is another one of the reasons I decided to retire. I had a hard time making myself read.

Stick up for your Principles

And be prepared for the assault on them because it will happen. Sometimes it's just easier to give in (give the Rx for Percocet, sign the Rx for a wheelchair, say they are disabled, say they can't go back to work) just to get them out of your office and not fight with them. You just get beaten down. Stay strong.

Accept Responsibility

Accept responsibility for your own actions. Don't blame others. If you screwed up, fess up.

Be Prepared

I call it John Wayne surgery. "Get in there and do what is right." Sometimes things happen (emergencies, something goes wrong), but you don't plan on it. And if you're prepared, it is far less likely. Spending time in preparation, I felt the surgery was mostly done. Then, I just had to do the plan that was already in my head. Surgery is mostly in the head (Preparation), less so in the hands (Performance). Preparation allowed me to be relaxed and confident. It was always tougher if I wasn't prepared.

You owe it to your patient. I could always tell when somebody was not prepared. They were slow and fiddled around trying to figure things out. Preparation makes for better surgery and better outcomes. It's a win-win.

Be Conservative

Don't try something new unless it solves a problem you are currently having. And then, still be cautious. There will always be something new. Is it better? New and approved is not necessarily new and improved. Let somebody else find out about the absolutely unanticipated problems. You just don't know what they will be until they happen. It's the law of unintended consequences.

I like to go in confident. I don't like experimenting on somebody, especially without their consent, which good studies have to do. You could decide to try a new prosthesis for a number of reasons, some good (seems like an improvement and it's cheaper), some not (getting paid to do it-really bad, the rep bought you lunch or took you golfing). If I was paid to do it, I would feel guilty. It wouldn't feel honest. Remember, if something doesn't go well, it wasn't because you experimented on them, especially without their knowledge.

If you want to do research, you should be set up for it. I think it should be done in university settings where they have the team and resources. In private practice, we don't have that. Most research projects in private practice are not for scientific study. It might be for a company and usually involves a per head fee to sign people up. I feel that is taking care of yourself, instead of taking care of the patient. It is the classic conflict of interest. I like to use the tried and true until long term studies (five years or more) to show it's safe and effective and I'm not on the wrong end of any new surprises. Be conservative.

Be able to say, "I Was Wrong."

Recognize Your Limitations

There will always be other people that are better than you are at certain procedures because they are just better or they do more of them or they have a system set up to handle all the problems that can occur. Sometimes they are just smarter. There is a Mayo Clinic for a reason.

Treat People Decently

It's just the right thing to do. I'm from Iowa and that's how we treat people. People from Iowa are genuine. What you see is what you get. They are genuinely interested in you and want to know more about you. They want to be helpful. This is important to me because it's the way I would like to be treated. That's what you do! You build a practice and have people like you. (Some don't care, but most people do.)

This helped me help my patients because they sensed it. They came back. They told their friends. They trusted me. They let me schedule surgery on them, or their kids.

Take Care of Your Family

They are people too, arguably (hopefully) the most important in your life. They deserve priority for your time and efforts, not just money.

Be honest.

If you are loose with the truth, it will come around and bite you in the butt. Almost guaranteed. It may be painful up front, but it saves greater pain later.

Be fair.

Be nice.

Don't be mean.

Listen.

Don't cut off your patients at ten seconds. Remember, research has proven that letting them speak for just 60 seconds can make them claim you are the best doctor they've ever seen! And, they will be far less likely to sue you.

Listen to everybody. Show you are concerned about somebody else besides yourself.

Be on time.

Be humble.

Smile!

It's amazing how much better you are perceived by doing this simple maneuver. Try not to fake it too much.

Enjoy Yourself Along the Way

It makes no sense to be the richest guy in the cemetery.

Work-Life Balance

This is how you take care of your family. There is no such thing as, "I'm going to spend some quality time with my family this weekend." Nonsense. You can never predict when quality time will happen. You just have to spend quantity time so you will be there when the quality moments occur. Take vacations or you may never get to do all the things you talked about doing.

Cut Down on Stress

Stress takes a little chunk out of you every day you have it. More stress means more chunks. You can't avoid it. Our job is stressful. It's built into what we do. We help take care of people's health. But figure out ways to cut that down. Avoid the unnecessary things that you know stress you out (like lawyers, government, meetings, and certain people).

Get A Handle on Your Money

Keep money secondary to your core principles. Make it a means to the end, not the end you are striving for. Money is addictive. The more you get, the more you need or want. And it can change you. I've seen it. And those people are never happy. I learned this from the Dominicans. They are the happiest people I have ever met and they had nothing.

It's all about expectations. Don't make unrealistic expectations for yourself, just like you shouldn't for your patients. It only creates unhappiness.

Be in Practice with Good People

This is hard to do. You only know them a short time when you make this decision. Sometimes you just get lucky, or not.

Compartmentalize

Also, hard to do. It's hard to concentrate on your routine patients when you have just admitted the total knee replacement you did a month ago to the hospital with a florid infection and you know they are facing two to three more operations, IV antibiotics for six to eight weeks, and will be very lucky to have half as good a result as you both planned. But you've got to learn to do it.

Be Grateful

Appreciate everything.

Give Back

It helps you keep perspective on what's important. You bitch a lot less when you know you could have it a lot worse. This goes along with being appreciative. And, in this field, you really can make a difference.

The Big Decisions

You begin wrestling with these big decisions when you first decide to go to medical school and the commitment it takes to do that. Then, when you get in, you have to decide what field to go into. Surgical or nonsurgical? Then, as you are finishing your residency, what practice to join and where?

Here is where you decide to get married with perhaps a weekend courtship. But you also do this with decisions outside of medicine. Should I buy into this practice? Many times, you will look at a decision and come up with an equally good rationale for doing two things that are the polar opposite of each other. Then what do you do?

You will most often wrestle with this when deciding whether to do surgery on someone. Some decisions are pretty straightforward. The hard ones are the ones where the indications for surgery are not that obvious or there are confounding factors. Then, once you decide that surgery is the right thing to do, that starts another cavalcade of decisions.

You will also wrestle with this in keeping your practice from getting out of control. Mike MacMillan called it "running downhill." Best way to build a practice is one word-yes! But that is also how it can spin out of control. Will you work in this extra patient? Of course. Will you go see this consult for a diabetic foot infection in the hospital? Sure. Will you be on the Q&A committee? Oh, Okay. Will you take this day of call for me?

You will unexpectedly wrestle with this in business decisions. (Should we open a new office in this rapidly growing area?) There will be family decisions; should I get my ten year old a cell phone? Do I let my daughter stay overnight at a coed sleepover? Taking on debt; should we buy that nice house in the neighborhood we like?

This is where you go back to your standards, apply them and their principles then hope you are correct. Sometimes, you never know until it's all over. But, at least you are not beating yourself up. You "Made the best decision you could with the information you had at the time." It's easier to live with yourself if you have done that.

CHAPTER 12
KEY DECISIONS

Career Decisions

What Field to Go Into

Most people go into private practice where your main focus is treating patients. But if you have research aspirations, you may think about academic medicine at a university, or tertiary care center with fewer patient care responsibilities and more time and resources for research. It's difficult to do good quality research with the demands of private practice. The focus is different.

Medical Student Advice

I heard students for years, especially when I was in residency saying, "I really like surgery and would like to do it, but I just don't think I can get through the residency. And I don't want to work that hard." With good reason. It can be brutal. I would tell them "This is a fork in the road. Pick a surgical field only if you just have to do surgery. Not just that you would like to, you have to. If not, go into a nonsurgical field." It's too demanding (time, effort, the call, the responsibilities, the crap, the risk, the stress) if you aren't really unfulfilled if you don't do it.

Choose what you like. I wouldn't choose anything because of how lucrative it is. It's tough to be miserable for 40 years because you hate what you are doing just to make a better living. You can also never know what will happen to reimbursements in the future, so don't get yourself in $250K of debt that will be hard to repay if you choose pediatrics.

Where to Do Your Residency

Once you decide on your field, then you choose where you go for your residency. This will be determined primarily on your compatibility with the people in the program, the program's priorities, and if you think you and/or your family can tolerate where you will live for three to five years. (Do not choose a residency because of the city. You will have very little time to enjoy that place.) You want a good program that will teach you how to be a good doctor in the field you chose.

The Match

This is not entirely your decision because of "The Match." What is that? The Match refers to a system run by the National Resident Matching Program to place medical students into a residency program. There is actually an algorithm that determines who goes where. Each student interviews anywhere from six to ten programs. Then, they rank the programs they are willing to go to.

Likewise, each program ranks the students they interviewed that they would be willing to accept. Then, the students and the programs submit their list to a central computer that matches the rankings of each student to the rankings of the programs. Nobody knows (or is supposed to know) who goes where until the computer matches you to the program that has ranked you the highest.

Everybody in each class meets on March 17 (or close to it) and is given an envelope where they match. One minute, you have no idea where you are going. The next minute, you find out where you will spend the next three to five years of your life. And it's a decision that can often affect where you live for the rest of your life, who you marry, and your long-term friends. (It's a common occurrence to wind up practicing somewhere within a two-hour radius of where you did your residency.) It's the biggest decision in your life that you really don't have much control over. It's huge!

"YOU WHAT?" Decisions

Bad Decisions

Lots of bad decisions are made in medicine, as in life. Some don't matter or don't matter much. If you schedule too many patients, most everybody forgets the next day.

Some are important, but eventually resolve. You take the stitches out too early, the wound opens up a little, you change some dressings and no long-term problems, except maybe a wider scar.

There are terrible decisions that are monumental for a short time for you and the patient (you operate on the wrong leg), there is some worsening of the problem, but you both go back to relatively normal lives after the lawsuit and the penalties imposed by the state for wrong site surgery.

And there are the decisions that may not have been a bad decision at the time, maybe a small error in judgement, but the eventual consequences leave the patient with a vastly altered life or they even die. (You take the stitches out at the right time, the wound opens up all the way, they get a deep infection in their knee replacement, they go through multiple failed surgeries, they get a sepsis and have to have an amputation or even die. We have a term for that. It's called a train wreck.)

Sometimes you never know.

Humorous

There are not too many bad decisions that are funny, especially with patients. But some bad decisions in life can eventually become funny stories.

Hip drawings

We used to have conferences in residency every morning. Pre-op, fracture, tumor, pathology, biomechanics, post-op. The residents would present a clinical problem, what was done and a little tutorial on the problem and it's solution. My friend Mike MacMillan was an excellent artist and supplemented his presentations with salient sketches that enhanced our understanding of the problem. I, however, was not a good artist. But I wasn't going to let that stop me. I could do this. Bad decision.

That week my presentation was on hip osteotomy (cutting the hip bone to realign it) and I proceeded to draw a number of hip joints on the chalkboard. When I finished, it was dead silent. You could hear a scalpel drop. I thought, "They are impressed." Then our department chief said, "Chase, that looks like a bunch of penises impaled on sticks!"

The laughter that erupted was volcanic! Nothing could be accomplished in the rest of the conference because of the raucous laughter that kept interrupting whoever was speaking. They all called it, "The Dick on the Stick." The residents wouldn't let anybody erase my sketches from the board for weeks.

For years after, when anyone put a bad drawing on the board, the response was, "Well, it's not as bad as Chase." Quite a legacy, I left.

Sugar Ray Concert

Some of my worst decisions came as a parent. Parenting is the classic conundrum. I could not be called a cool parent. But I heard on the radio that "Sugar Ray" was going to be in concert at Hardrock Live. I had heard a Sugar Ray song on the radio and liked it and I thought, "I'll take my daughters to that. It's an activity we can do together."

I got four tickets, but my middle daughter Sarah was going to be out of town with my wife, so I told my freshman in high school, Megan, "You can invite a friend." The friend she invited was the daughter of the director of the Child Protective Team at the Trauma Center in town. I should have known something was up when, as I was telling the story of us going to the concert, the Anesthesiologist said, "Dr Chase, how much do you know about Sugar Ray?" I replied, "I like that song he has on the radio." The response was, "Ohhhh, I see."

We go to the concert with the two freshmen, plus my eight-year-old daughter, Anna, and Sugar Ray plays the one song I know, "Someday." Then immediately after, he goes into this loud, head banging punk rock set. What's worse was, a "mosh pit" with crowd surfing immediately started up and I see my two daughters, eight and fourteen, accompanied by the girl with parents whose job it is to protect children from injury, head toward the mosh pit, where she could be dropped on her head by a bunch of rowdy punk rockers.

I was aghast and grabbed them and said, "We are leaving! Now!!" I could feel the knives that were coming out of their eyes hitting me in the back of the head all the way home from that one song concert. Parenting fail. One of many.

Work-Life Balance Decisions

Many of your biggest decisions will revolve around the lure of money. After years of self-denial during pre-med, med school, and residency (that's 12-15 years after high school), you may be very tempted to finally reward yourself and satisfy that pent-up demand for material goods you could never afford before. And you should, to an extent. Remember I said money can change you, especially if you get sucked into the comparison game. Just keep your perspective because, if you don't, it can overtake you in insidious ways. How busy do you allow your practice to get? Everybody wants to be busy. You trained for a long time and you want to be able to use your skills. "I want to help people," is the quote from your med school interviews. Now is your chance. And, you have debts to pay.

You also want to do some things, like travel or start a family. These things have a better chance of happening if you are busy. So, everybody wants to be busy. But, it's slow at first. Nobody knows you. You depend upon the group for referrals. But it doesn't take long.

Then you are getting busier and busier. At some point, you have to decide how much is enough for you. Lots of factors there. Everybody has different capacities. Some of my partners could see 60-80 patients a day. I don't know how, but they did. I never could do that and feel I was doing a good job. This is a big decision that your happiness and contentment depends on. Make that decision yourself. Don't just let it happen and then be chronically stressed.

To Stay in the Practice

You think the big decision is where to start your practice. It is. But a bigger one is, do you stay in that practice? You never know, especially with such a brief courting time. Some perfectly nice people in your interview may have been acting. Then you see what they're really like under day to day stresses. And they may not be quite so nice. They may be real asses. Maybe they wanted someone new to share call with (or take the brunt of it), but don't want to share referrals, especially for the lucrative procedures. Maybe they stack the appointment algorithm their way.

Most places have a one to two-year trial employment before deciding to let you become a partner. This is when you decide to make a financial commitment and buy in to the assets of the practice. You now become a full partner (whatever that is.) Is it equal to the senior guy or will you always be a second-class citizen? Becoming a partner is the marriage equivalent of having kids. It is much easier to part ways before that big milestone.

So, you decide to buy in. This usually involves a large financial investment that you inevitably have to borrow. You may be adding that to your already sizable school debts. Big decisions. Everyone, at some time, wonders if the grass is greener on the other side. Inevitably, there will be bumps in the road. Some small (potholes), some larger (detours in your planned route), and some may be monstrous (like sinkholes that swallow your house and street). Are these bumps insurmountable? Here, you can follow Ann Landers advice, "Are you better off with them or without them?"

If the answer is "Without," then you start looking for another practice. A big setback and very painful. Now you have to start the whole process over and you do lose a fair amount of ground.

When to Retire

Eventually, after you have been in practice for a while, you start thinking about hanging it up. Here are a few things to consider. If you love what you are doing, keep doing it. Just make sure you haven't been putting off a bunch of things you like to do, that you plan to do, "when you retire." You may never get to them. You could die or become infirm, so you can't travel.

Or, you could retire the very day the entire world shuts down due to a Covid-19 virus pandemic. That's what happened to me. At this writing, September 2020, I still don't know the difference between retirement and house arrest.

Couple of old sayings that ring true:

You should retire while you are still valued, but not yet pitied.

You should retire when you have enough and you have just about had enough. This was pretty good advice for me. I had enough so I got out. I have not regretted it for a minute. I miss some of the people, but none of the nonsense involved with being in a medical practice.

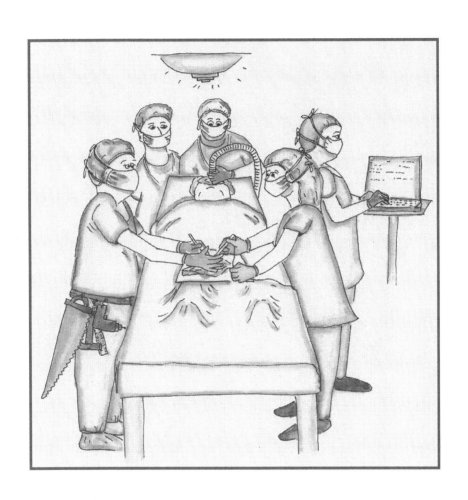

CONCLUSION

I hope you enjoyed sharing my journey through a career of highs and lows, as well as hearty laughs and genuine heartaches. Despite some considerable struggles getting there, and then surviving, my career in medicine (and Orthopaedic surgery) has been very gratifying, very rewarding, and a lot of fun.

If you are on the path to a life in medicine, I wish you all the best! And I hope I've given you some useful tips and food for thought to make it the best life possible.

The secret to having a great life (inside or outside of medicine) is to remember to do three things:

1. Be conscientious and responsible. Take good care of your patients.

2. Treat people decently. Take good care of people, most especially your family.

3. Enjoy yourself along the way. Take good care of yourself.

Do the things that will make you a success based on your own criteria, not somebody else's.

It's your life. Make it a great life in the medical field!

ABOUT THE AUTHOR

John Chase is a recently retired Orthopaedic surgeon who found himself with plenty of time (thanks to the Covid-19 house arrest) and information about the practice of medicine he wanted to pass along.

Dr. Chase attributes his values to growing up in Iowa, and his solid fund of knowledge from receiving his undergraduate degree from Iowa State University and his medical degree from the University of Iowa.

Orthopaedic Residency at the University of Florida rounded out his academic and surgical preparation for a career in Orthopaedic surgery, focusing on knee and ankle problems.

He is married to Marian, an ARNP (Advanced Registered Nurse Practitioner) who focuses her efforts clinically to help patients with chronic diseases better manage those diseases through what they ingest, as opposed to throwing more medicines at it.

What has driven John's efforts throughout the years, and still does, is developing, supporting, and enjoying his three daughters: Megan, Sarah, and Anna. His greatest fulfillment is seeing them turning out to be independent, competent, and enjoyable people to be around. They are starting families with great guys he couldn't be happier with.

John considers his family to be the personal legacy he is passing on and this book is the professional side of his legacy.

WANTED

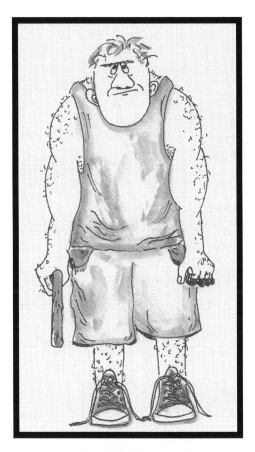

SOMEDUDE

Beware of SomeDude! He lurks at times when you
mind your own business and seeks to cause injury.
See page 40 for a full description.

Made in the USA
Columbia, SC
25 April 2023